I wrote this book in memory of my son, kaiden Rhys Paul cooper who was "incompatible with life", born on 31st October 2018 at 2.59pm.
Who's life was brief, yet still a gift.

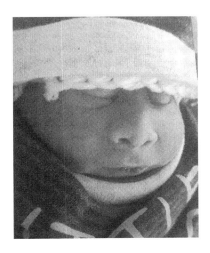

Introduction

"Incompatible with life" a term I first heard on the 25th of June 2018.

That was the day I found out my child, a child I had not even met yet was going to die.

I noticed the specialist becoming more and more quiet and more serious, "have you ever heard of Anencephaly "he said.

I once heard someone say grief is not a life sentence but a life passage. It is the one common human experience we all have at one time or another, but we never expected it to be the death of a child, did we?

if anybody reading this book has lost a child or have been affected by the loss of a child you are now discovering that grieving this loss is the hardest thing you have ever done.

This loss is feared amongst all parents and an unimaginable loss, unimaginable until it happens to you.

People refer to it as "the worst that can happen "and that is exactly what it feels like.

completely new area surrounded by people I have never even seen.

In my first year of secondary school one of my male maths teachers said very inappropriate things to me every time we seen each other or when I was in his class, ever since than I had my guard up and an I developed an extremely bad attitude towards all the students and the teachers.

I did not have very many friends in secondary school, nor did I have anybody to talk to, this experience hurt me and affected me deeply.

At the start of third year, I personally decided that it would be best for me to transfer to a new school, I hated where I was, I never wanted to go in. the new school was in my area and there was plenty of familiar faces and people I knew also, I felt great.

It was a fresh start for me, I joined my new school on the 1st of February 2018 and this is when my story truly began.

Finding out I was pregnant

On the 10th of April 2018, I was on my lunchbreak from school which lasted thirty minutes, I was already two weeks late on my period, my periods were always regular, I was already starting to worry that I was pregnant, I remember I just kept telling myself that I was not "I can't be pregnant" is all I kept on telling myself after all I was only fourteen years old. On that day, my mam picked me up from school for my lunchbreak, as soon as I got home and walked up the stairs my mam handed me a pharmacy bag, she did not say anything she just walked away, I already knew what was in the bag before I even opened it, this was when I really started to panic, my anxiety arose, I could feel my heart trying to jump out of my chest.

I was not even in a relationship, it was so unexpected, after all I was young and dumb, neither of us used protection, what was I expecting? A new television.

, I clearly just never thought of it in any other way rather than just having "sex".

Right then and there I found out I was five weeks pregnant. My mam cried and sent me back to school, I remember sitting in class thinking to myself "what the hell" it still did not sink in yet, I was worried sick to go home after school when my dad would be home from work.

Coping with my pregnancy news at 14

When I first discovered I was pregnant, I needed to accept the fact that I was in shock, with feelings ranging from being thrilled and delirious to be negative and confused.

I was also aware of my options as a woman, but personally I would never turn to abortion or termination, but as I said I was aware of my options.

I decided to carry my baby.

With the initial shock and thoughts going through my head I knew that it was just a phase that I knew I should try and accept, and to wait for the most intense emotions that have surfaced to subside after a few days.

Allowing myself to experience the rollercoaster of emotions, accepting them and letting them go as they would.

I was aware of the feelings that would trigger actual physical reactions in me, I paid special attention to those ones, I wrote all these feelings and emotion down in a private notebook I kept hidden in my wardrobe so that after a few days or so I could reference them and pick out the ones that were more important and the ones that were less important.

Although it was challenging, I tried to put aside outside issues, such as education and family issues and opinions, and I tuned into whatever was in my gut, my gut feeling, I wrote this down privately also.

Every time a gut feeling arose, I focused on it, I was truthful with myself, and I wrote all of it down in my little notebook.

Everybody has visions of how their life would be and if they could attain the best, a life they would feel to be close to perfection. I was afraid to evaluate these visions, I have always seen myself finishing school with a masterly leaving cert and getting into one of the finest colleges in Ireland, to become a doctor, nurse, or midwife, but also, I knew that not everyone accomplishes their perfect vision of life, what is the perfect life anyway?

I learned that even women who have planned pregnancies in what appears to be in the perfect situation, in terms of health, relationship and money all go through fears of not being a good enough mother.

On top of that other fears such as what if your child has a birth defect? Or if something goes wrong during pregnancy or childbirth, also maybe feeling overwhelmed by the prospect of giving birth.

The fear I had of my baby, my child having a birth defect became a reality, what I feared so much for the foetus inside of me became a living nightmare.

We cannot control all aspects of our lives and as I moved through this process, I was honest about what my gut feeling was telling me, this was my true personal psychology for dealing with my unplanned pregnancy at fourteen years old.

Visualization is a helpful tool for many life situations.

I visualized myself in my home with my new baby, thinking to myself how did it feel? I visualised myself walking to my local shop or café with my new baby in his or her pram. I visualised whatever seemed natural to me, this triggered more genuine gut feelings.

I talked to those around me, those who I knew to be non-judgemental, supportive, and balanced.

This type of support was important to me to have, and I was an incredibly lucky little girl to have it. As I expressed, I had an incredibly happy childhood, this made it a bit easier for me to accept this surprise into my life, I have seen my mother and father being so loving and supportive to me and my siblings through our whole lives; it may not be as bad as I was thinking after all, I thought to myself. I wanted to be the type of mother my mam was And still is, that in my eyes she was the perfect definition of a mother figure. The initial shock was starting to ease off, but even after this I still had some nagging self-doubts, as any new mother, or first-time mother would.I remembered that there is no definition of a Perfect parent, maybe a visualization, yes, but not A definition.I also realized that there is no time limit or a set age to become a mother nor to be a good one.

One of my biggest fears was how my immediate family and extended family would react, I was afraid of the way both my grandmothers, my aunt and uncles would respond, what if they would think different of me?.

I wanted to tell everybody straight away just to get it over and done with but also, I wanted to sort out the way I felt, until I got my own head around the whole scenario.

I still needed to get my head around the fact that I was growing a tiny human inside of me. My mam and dad told me to wait until I had my First ultrasound that would take place when I was About twelve weeks pregnant before I told anybody else.

I knew other members of my family, and Extended family or friends may react in unexpected ways to my news, one of the main reasons being my young age, I was only a baby myself. "Babies having babies" as some people like to say about teen moms.

I was just nervous about the whole ordeal, I just wanted to be accepted, like I have wanted to be my whole life, I wanted everyone to accept my news just like I had.

Changes in my body

Around three weeks after my missed period I started feeling nauseous and I was getting sick, I started to google early pregnancy symptoms, I read and studied it, I wanted to understand what was going on inside my body.

I learned that the sickness I was experiencing is common in early pregnancy for many women, it is also commonly known as "morning sickness" but feeling this sickness does not necessarily happen in the morning, it can happen anytime during the day.

I seemed to just get it in the morning time right after my breakfast.

I also experienced extreme fatigue and tiredness, I felt it extremely hard for me to do my usual day routines, such as getting up for school, sitting in class, doing my homework, even showering, and getting out of my bed to get dressed, I started falling asleep during classes and it was extremely difficult for me to complete precious schoolwork needed for my junior certificate.

I read that it is quite common to feel tired especially in the first twelve weeks also known as the first trimester.

Hormonal changes were taking place in my body, these hormonal changes made me feel tired, nauseous, and emotional, my breasts also became larger, and they stood up more. These changes in my body scared me, they were strange and very new to me, just like they would be for any first-time mother, but I knew this was all part of this new and magical journey into motherhood and to bringing my little human into this world.

After school one day I decided to go over to a friend's house, we did our homework together, and laughed together, it was something positive to take my mind off things.

It was a summers day, so I wore a t-shirt and white shorts, we had fun, I felt like a normal teenager.

My mam picked me up later that day as I was getting in to the car she looked at me with terror telling me to turn around , I was confused , I said "why what's wrong" , my mam said that there was blood on my shorts , I ran back in to my friends toilet and I checked myself but there was nothing on my underwear nor nothing there when I wiped myself , I got the fright of my life , it was a fake tan stain ,as I only put on fake tan on the night before . In that moment I feared that I had lost my baby.

I started leaking milk from my boobs also when I was just 17 weeks pregnant. I knew that is what would happen my breasts after birth, but I did not know that it could happen before birth. When I first seen my breasts leak, I did not know what was happening or what it was, it was nigh time and I was getting ready for bed, I remember just screaming into my mam and she explained what it was. The doctors in the hospital said its perfectly fine and it can happen before birth.

First doctor's appointment

At around eight weeks pregnant, I had my first doctor appointment with my general practitioner.

My mam brought me to my local clinic to notify them that I was pregnant, as I needed to get a referral sheet that I needed to fill out to send to my maternity hospital, for them to make me an appointment for my first ultrasound.

At the doctor's office my general practitioner asked me for the date of the first day of my last menstrual cycle, to get an understanding of how far long pregnant I was, she than measured my tiny bump and told me that I was showing correctly for how far long gone I was.

The age of sexual consent in Ireland is seventeen years old, as I was only fourteen years old my doctor had to get in touch with social workers as the father of my baby was 17 which as I said is the age of consent, but I made sure my doctor knew it was consensual, it was just protocol.

I still did not really feel a connection to my small baby yet, but things were starting to look up for me, those bd nagging thoughts were disappearing slowly but surely out of my head, I was starting to feel good about my pregnancy and I was getting excited to hopefully see my small baby kicking about inside my belly in an ultrasound.

I was aware that one in four pregnancies end up in a miscarriage, I prayed to God that my pregnancy would not be the one in four, that I would get to see my baby for the first time. Two weeks after my doctor's appointment we got the letter from my maternity hospital with my appointment on it for my first scan which was then scheduled for the end of May.

My First encounter with death and grief

27th April 2018, that was the day I found out that my great-grandmother kitty passed away, my great-grandmother suffered Alzheimer's and dementia, the past few years before her passing were very tough on her, no matter how many things she forgot, one thing she never forgot was her family, she was the heart of the family.

My great-grandmother passed away just several days after her eighty ninth birthday.

I was always awfully close with my great-grandmother.

I never even got to tell her that she was going to be a great-great grandmother.

My family tell me now that it was her time to go so, she could look after me, and that she was waiting for Kaiden.

The whole way through my pregnancy, every time I looked outside to my back garden, there was a robin red breast that would sit on the branch that hung over my back wall and it would sit their looking into me, I now believe that the robin red breast was my nanny

looking over me telling me everything is going to be okay.
My baby would have been her first great-great grandchild.

My First ultrasound

On the 29th of May 2018, I was twelve weeks and one day pregnant.

My mum made sure to wake me up exceedingly early for my appointment, so that we would not be late.

I remember just bursting out of my bed, after all that was the day that I would see my baby for the first time, it would be the first time where I would see my baby kick around, I would be able to hear and look at my child's heartbeat.

The first ultrasound you will have is for your doctor to confirm a viable and healthy pregnancy, this will also allow them to determine your due date more accurately as estimating the first day of your last menstrual cycle does not always prove to be reliable, this test also lets your doctor know early how many babies are growing.

Ultrasounds are a regular part of pregnancy, but the first one is incredibly special.

Your first ultrasound will be the first time you will get to see your growing little one, even if they do only look like a tiny tadpole, it will also be the first time you will hear and see his or her heartbeat.

The first twelve-week ultrasound was important to me as I knew it would include an anatomy scan of my baby.

On the way to the maternity hospital for my appointment, we stopped off at McDonalds and my mam bought me and her breakfast, I just remember puking out of the car window, we laughed about it, we were happy.

Firstly, when we went into the hospital, we had to go to the reception to pick up my file, we than sat and waited as I needed to get blood tests done, after that than I had to go into a room without my mother and answer a few questions just to keep on record in my file.

In the waiting area for the ultrasound, I just remember sitting there looking at all the heavily pregnant women, trying to push and show off my little bump, in that moment I felt proud.

All I wanted was to just see my baby, I felt as if I could not wait anymore, but I also remembered how nervous I was, and how scared I was knowing that there could be any possibility that there was could have been something wrong with my baby.

I just wanted to hear the words "everything is okay".
I made sure I said all my prayers the night before.
I prayed to God, but I also prayed to my nanny.
I remember having my legs and my fingers crossed as I sat in the waiting room, I was praying non-stop, all I wanted was for everything to just be okay.
We were than brought into the scanning room, I could not stop shaking with my nerves, my head felt heavy, my palms on my hand were sweating profusely and my knees were weak.
I could not help but look at very move the midwife made, I remember staring at her to see was she looking at my scan in any sort of way that indicated that something was wrong.
I truly did not understand the true meaning of perfection until I seen my sweet child on that screen, I could see his legs moving up and down, and his arms moving side to side as if he were waving at me and his nanny.
It was hard to believe that that was my baby I was looking at, he was tiny, like a peanut as I called him.

Me and my mam were told everything we wanted to hear, that everything was okay, we were told everything was perfect.

The only thing the midwife told us was that my baby was measuring a bit small, just one week behind my estimated due date, it was not a big issue she said, that I had nothing to worry about, instead she put me down as eleven weeks and one day pregnant instead of twelve.

She than booked me in for an appointment for two weeks' time for a re-dating scan to see did he grow to my correct dates, but for the moment my estimated due date was the 24th of December 2018, Christmas eve.

She printed off two pictures for me from the ultrasound.

Me and my mam made sure to ring my father and my family to tell them everything was okay, that my baby was okay, we decided than to tell my extended family and friends, I also posted about my pregnancy on social media.

I remember sitting in the kitchen with my mam and my dad waiting for my brothers to get home from school so we could tell them my news.

They got home and my mam told them to sit around the table, I than told them I had some news and I put the scan pictures of kaiden on the table and they all looked at my mam and said are we having a new brother or sister, we all laughed, and my mam said, "no that's Laurens's baby, you are going to have a new niece or nephew". They all jumped up out of the chairs they were sitting on, and they all gave me a big hug.

I was not afraid anymore, I was proud, it felt normal to me now.

My friends and family all were extremely supportive, they were all happy for me.

I remember the next day my nanny collected me from school with my mama, and she just smiled and gave me the biggest hug in the world, that there was one of those special moments in life where you snapshot it and frame it inside your memory.

Finding out something was wrong

On the 19^{th of} June 2018, I was fourteen weeks pregnant, I had just turned fifteen years old five days prior, this was the day of my re-dating scan.

I was going to get to see my baby kick and wave again.

I felt as if during those two weeks I had gotten a bond with my baby, seeing him for the first time really helped.

I started talking to him whilst holding my small bump, I also started to sing him songs every night, "you are my sunshine" being one of my favourites.

I loved bonding with my baby.

My baby bump just kept on getting bigger and bigger.

I started being confident in myself, I than fell in love with my pregnant self, my body, and my new baby.

My child I had not even met yet I loved more than the moon and the stars.

The midwife greeted us with a friendly handshake, and she introduced herself, it was a different woman to the last time.

I laid down on the table, she than put the ultrasound gel on my stomach, and she than began to measure and examine my baby.

He looked so perfect just how we had seen him for.

Once again, he was kicking about with his tiny legs.

He was not only a tiny dot anymore, but his features were also so much clearer than before, they really do grow in the blink of an eye.

Me, my mama, and the midwife giggled as we looked at him, he was so energetic, the midwife said he was like a little monkey.

We than listened to my child's beautiful heartbeat, it was like music to my ears.

Next thing I know the midwife turned to quiet, the screen turned black, I could not see my baby anymore. she began to look more closely, and she looked more serious also, in fact the whole room went quiet.

I knew something was wrong, I just could not understand what, we had just listened to his heartbeat.

I just remember saying to her "if there is something wrong, you have got to tell me, because your quiet is making me really nervous".

As soon as the technician got to my baby's head and stomach, she knew it was not right, I just remember her turning around to face me and she picked my hand up and held it and told me that her and the hospital team was going to help me through this, I still did not have a clue what was going on.

I looked at my mam and she was sitting there with tears rolling down her face, I did not know why.

The midwife pointed out that there was something seriously wrong, she than zoomed in to my babies' stomach and she told me it appeared like his liver was growing outside of his abdomen instead of inside.

She then went to have another look at my baby's head and explained that his bone structure was not developing properly.

I did not cry; I do not understand why I did not. To be honest it was almost like an out of body experience for me because here I am looking at my sons' silhouette and he looked perfect to me, everything she was describing went against what I felt like I was seeing.

The technician left the room to get another colleagues opinion, she told me and my mam the exact same thing about my sweet child.

As a teenager myself, all I knew and really understood was miscarriage, once you got past twelve weeks gestation, I classed myself "out of the woods".

Seeing my little boy so active, that is why I thought she was having problems with the measurements because he was moving around like mad.

That illusion was soon shattered, and my life divided into "before" and "after".

This was truly a defining moment for me, perhaps the most defining moment of my life.

The technician than left the room and gave me and my mam a moment.

I remember silence, just silence, it was that quiet I would say if you listened close enough you would have been able to hear the teardrops running down my mother's face and onto the floor.

I did not know what to say, what to do, what to think nor how to feel.

The only word to describe me was emotionless, I was emotionless.

The technician than came back into the room and she took me by the hand and helped me up off the table, she looked me into my two eyes and told me she was so sorry.

It was true, my baby did have serious problems.

The technician than escorted me and my mam out of the room, and then led us out of the staff exit.

I felt as if my heart was ripped out of my chest and thrown onto the floor.

They then told me that I was to come back on the Friday to attend an appointment with a foetal medicine doctor and the best thing to do was not to panic until we seen him, until we knew exactly what was wrong with my child.

That car journey home was something I wish to never experience again, nothing was said, not a word, what could have been said?

I did not know how I was going to tell my dad that something was seriously wrong with his grandchild. How was I going to tell my brothers that something was wrong with their niece or nephew?

My heart was completely shattered into a million pieces, but after all I still had hope, in times like that what else could you turn to, I turned to God as well, throughout my whole pregnancy with kaiden was when I truly grew my relationship with God, praying became a daily routine for me.

We got home and told my dad what was said at the scan.

Me, my mama, and my dad just hugged each other, my dad squeezed us into him as we cried.

My dad stayed strong for us no matter how hard it was on him, he made sure he was always there for me and his family. He always shad and that is what he continues to do.

.

Appointment with the foetal medicine doctor

On Friday 22nd June 2018, I was fourteen weeks and four days pregnant, it was time for me to go back to the hospital to see the specialist but this time it was not exciting, I was not ecstatic, I was not jumping out of my bed, yes, sure I was happy to be getting to see my baby again, but I was scared, nervous and I was miserable.

I really did not want to go and see and hear that my perfect baby had so many problems, we were finding out what was wrong with him, I felt doomed, what if I found out there was nothing that could be done, how could I have any hope than, I felt as if all my hope would be lost and that was the only thing keeping my head up.

We got to the hospital, picked up my chart and waited, I would not say patiently for twenty minutes, I than heard med us09# with a handshake and a big infection smile, he then told my mam to take a seat.

I laid down onto the table.
The specialist turned to me and told me he was deeply sorry that we had to meet under these circumstances.
He turned on the screen and put the probe on my stomach, he let us hear his heartbeat.
He was looking around at the screen mumbling "ah yes, yes" to himself.
Not even five minutes passed by, and the screen was turned off.
He said he agrees with the two technicians, that there is something abnormally wrong with my child.
He explained to me and my mother that my baby had a spine defect, a heart defect, an abdominal wall defect and a head (skull) defect, he then began to tell us that his liver and his bowel was growing outside of his abdominal wall, he did not have a diagnosis yet, but he did say that these three abnormalities usually occur when there is something chromosomally wrong with babies.
I than proceeded to ask him" what was going to happen from here?".
He replied that he wanted me to come back for a procedure called a "amniocentesis" on the following Friday.

Amniocentesis - a medical procedure used in prenatal diagnosis of chromosomal abnormalities in which a small amount of amniotic fluid, which contains foetal tissues, is sampled from the amniotic sac surrounding the developing baby.

It was an option for me, I did not know what to do with all honesty as there was a chance that my water could break during the procedure resulting in a miscarriage, I did not want to chance that, but then again what if there could be a cure for what my baby had.

My mind was so confused, and I was heartbroken, the specialist told me I did not have to get it done if I did not want to, we could just wait to see how my baby develops.

I finally decided that I would get the amniocentesis, the chance of miscarriage was exceedingly small, but still a possibility, I wanted to know what was going on, I was sick and tired with not knowing anything, I needed conclusion in whatever way that was.

the diagnosis

The night before the 29th of June, I could not sleep, I was up all-night crying hysterically knowing that the next day could have been the last day I spent with my baby being inside of me and alive, and it would have been my choice, my fault, I just wanted to know what was wrong.

I prayed to God all night long.

I kneeled on the end of my bed with my hands cupping each other begging for a miracle, apologising for all the bad I have ever done in my life.

I wondered why?

how This could be happening to my baby?

My child who was innocent of sin.

The morning of the 29th, I was not excited, I was nervous, distressed but hopeful.

It played on my mind; I still was not sure that this was the right decision for me and my unborn child.

I was fifteen weeks and four days pregnant; I did not want it to end.

As I was walking into my maternity hospital looking at all the happy pregnant women with their husbands and partners with smiles on their faces, it is like I felt some sort of anger against them for having a healthy and happy pregnancy.

Why couldn't I have that?

I was having a happy pregnancy, but not a healthy one., especially with what was said in my appointment that I was just about to walk in to.

Once again, I was sitting in the waiting room worried, distressed, the waiting room was filled with pregnant woman who were smiling and laughing with their partners, that is all I wished I were doing … sitting their smiling and laughing with my mam.

Instead, my legs were shaking, my palms were sweating profusely, then my name was called" Lauren cooper", I felt as if I was getting up out of my seat in slow motion, that all this worry and panic was dragging me down.

He did not bring me into an ultrasound room, but a conference room, a room with just a sofa and chairs, he then sat us down.

My specialist began to speak with his assistant sat beside him.

"I have been thinking about your baby and your situation over the past week and think I have a diagnosis".
"Have you ever heard of anencephaly" he said.

Anencephaly- an absence of a major portion of the brain, skull, and scalp, that occurs during   embryonic development. It is a cephalic disorder that results from a neural tube defect that occurs when the head end of the neural tube fails to close usually around the 23rd and 26th day following conception.

This was the diagnosis of what was wrong with his head. But what about his abdomen? He then followed to ask me" have I ever heard of an omphalocele".

Omphalocele- is a birth defect in which an infant's intestines or other abdominal organs are outside of the body because of a hole in the belly button. The organs are covered by a thin layer of tissue and can be easily seen.

The specialist than began to say that he believed that these two defects could be caused by a chromosomal defect, called trisomy 18 (Edward syndrome).

Trisomy 18 (Edward syndrome)- is a genetic disorder caused by the presence of all or part of an extra 18th chromosome. most people with the syndrome die during the foetal stage; infants who survive experience serious defects and commonly live for short periods of time.

After that conversation I was so numb, emotionless, as if I were in the middle of a blur, all I heard was "your baby is not viable for life, your baby is going to die, your baby should be dead".

I was then told most babies with anencephaly alone usually end up in early miscarriage as they are not viable for life.

The specialist was baffled and confused as to why my baby was still alive.

He told me that my baby will most likely pass away before the third trimester.

He proceeded to ask me did I want to continue to get the amniocentesis, but I refused as we had my baby's diagnosis, did not want to take any more risks, I was so determined to make it to the third trimester.

My specialist offered me two choices, termination or to carry my baby to term.

I chose to carry my baby to term, even though he was not "compatible with life".

Life is a gift, a baby is not a mistake, my baby was a gift to me and most of all a miracle.

For termination I would have to travel to England, I knew that it was not going to be an option for me, I was going to give my baby life in whatever god intended that life to be, all I could do was pray for a miracle.

I could barely comprehend what I was hearing. Everything seemed to be moving in slow motion. I had to tell myself to breath, after all I was in disbelief.

Maybe the doctor had made a mistake? after all he never did any testing to prove his diagnosis.

How was I going to tell my dad, my family, my brothers?

This baby was my first child, my brothers first nephew and my parents first grandchild. I felt guilty in some sort of way.

The more the doctor talked, the harder it was to hold back the tears, it felts as if the room was spinning around me; in that moment time stood still as I tried to comprehend what he was trying to tell me. I tried not to get to upset, it would make it real.

I wanted to give the doctor the chance to tell me that there was something that he could do, but that chance never came, there was no cure, there was nothing that him nor anybody could do to save my baby.

I turned my head to look at my mother sitting in the chair wringing her hands with her solemn with a scared look on her face.

It was incredibly difficult. What was there to say to one another? my baby was dying and there was nothing me, my mama, my family, or the specialist could do about it, there was nothing anybody could do to save my baby.

We went out into the corridor of the hospital, and I collapsed to the floor in tears, we had to walk by a bunch of other pregnant women who were on their way for an ultrasound or waiting on an ultrasound who looked at me with such terror.

The only thing I could think to do was to just grab and hug my mom while I sobbed into her arms in the middle of the hospital car park.

We than drove home, I really do not know how I did not kill myself on the way.

I could not process what the hospital had just told me.

How could this child of mine be fatally ill? Why was this happening to me? I could not put it together in my mind.

I could not stop what was going on, there was nothing I could do to stop it.

It felt so unfair.

At the appointment he explained that one in every 100,000 babies born have this condition.

The cause of this condition was unknown but that low levels of folic acid can be a contributing factor. It all felt like just one big sick joke.

The months and weeks to follow were exceedingly difficult.

The weeks following finding out that my baby was going to live was terrifying. I stayed in bed all day just wondering why? I was annoyed at God, why did he send me the most precious baby just to take him back.

God never gave my baby a chance in life, but I now see why.

I felt so alone, I was by myself not knowing all my family were there for me, I pulled away from the people who were there for me, they were struggling as well, they were hurting too.

I prayed and I prayed, that is all I could do.

I hoped that God would hear me out, and that he would answer my prayers, that maybe the doctors could have been wrong.

I soon realised God had different plans for my baby, for this angel of mine.

How could my first scan be fine, and everything was perfect, and we rang everyone with good news, to being told my baby had serious problems and having to ring friends and family to tell them my baby was going to die.

I was angry at this country.

There was extraordinarily little information online, but we gathered up all we could in the hope of finding someone somewhere who survived this condition, a new medical treatment, anything that could save my babies life, but we found nothing, my baby was going to die, and I was left with no choice but to carry my baby to term and bury him or to have my pregnancy and baby terminated early. My baby was going to die no matter what I did and that was something I was going to have to accept.

I felt as if I was being tortured, I still do. Medically speaking, the pregnancy went as normally as any other for the next couple of weeks. I would visit the hospital every four weeks, but nothing would change, my baby was still sick.

Emotionally, though it was exceedingly difficult, I was carrying a terminally ill baby at fifteen years old.
Feeling my baby move inside of me, bonding with him, falling in love with him, something so precious and important to me …. Yet knowing I would not get to keep him and that I most likely would not have got to see him alive. I felt as if my heart was being ripped out of my chest.

When they told me poor kaiden was a girl

On the 27th of June, we had a follow up appointment with the specialist which was two weeks after the diagnosis. I was seventeen weeks pregnant. seventeen weeks gestation is when some doctors can tell you the gender of the baby by ultrasound or earlier if done by blood test or amniocentesis.

I decided to give it a chance and I asked my specialist if he could tell me the gender of my baby.

He proceeded to do the ultrasound and he smiled and told me that he was 90% sure I was having a baby girl.

More than 80% of cases with anencephaly usually occur withing girls.

I was thrilled to think I was having a daughter; we rang everyone telling them good news for once, it was a bit of light after all the darkness. He made sure to give me lots of scan pictures from the ultrasound. Everything was still the same with my poor baby's health. But with that my baby boy still had that beautiful heartbeat, he still kicked like crazy, and I would take videos catching him in the act for memories to cherish forever, I still watch and cherish them even today.

After the appointment me and my mam headed down to the shopping centre where we bought a frame which said baby girl on it, we put the scan pictures from that day in it, we also bought a scrap book, I wanted to make memories with my baby and take pictures and put them in my scrapbook with little messages, it was special for me to do this. It hurt me that all I was buying was a scrapbook and not cots and nappies, things that I should have been buying.

I should have been running around the baby aisle picking out girly clothes and things for my babies' arrival, but instead I was picking out his coffin, I had to decide whether I wanted to bury or cremate him and picking out what type of flowers I wanted at his funeral, I had to pick out my child's burial outfit. yes, that hurt like hell, but do you know what hurt the most? That I did all this whilst I could feel my baby kick and move inside of me. I felt like the evilest person in the world.

Crying into my parent's arms became my normal way of falling asleep which would happen multiple times a night. When I would wake up for ten seconds before my bran would fully switch on and I remembered what was happening, I felt normal, then I would realise what was happening and I would break down again and again. I felt as if a part of me was dying, and I could not fix it.

Night-time was the time where my baby would kick around and move around the most. Feeling my baby move was a love/hate for me. Every kick or flutter broke my heart, it was a constant reminder of what I was going to lose, but every time my baby was quiet, I would freak out, I feared that something had happened him, it would put me in a state of panic until he would start moving again. In my mind I was living everyday with my baby like it was our last, any day could have been his last, that was the scary part.

One night I got a major scare, he had not moved for a good while and as I thought about it more, it had been hours since I last felt him move, I told my mam and we went straight to the emergency room in a panic, I proceeded to tell the nurse everything. I asked if I could have an ultrasound done, which it was done and it turned out that my baby was perfectly fine, he was just asleep, I seen his beautiful heart beating which put my mind at so much ease, I was reassured, I was a paranoid mess, but what did I expect, my baby could be taken from me at any time, my baby that I so long to hold.

Anything could happen to my baby, anywhere, any place or any time, and that is what scared my most the way through my pregnancy.

Sitting my junior certificate

On the fifteenth of June 2018, I sat my junior certificate, I was four months pregnant, I still suffered with my sickness but not as extreme. Every day I went in and sat every single one of my exams with pride, the only downfall was my sickness, therefore I had to sit my exams in a room by myself with a teacher supervising me.

Every morning before one of my exams my mama would buy me a hash brown sandwich, with no butter or sauce, that was one of my biggest cravings but not my weirdest.

My first Bereavement counselling meeting

On the 20th of June 2018 I had my first ever meeting with a bereavement counsellor, she was in my maternity hospital and my specialist referred me to her and said that she would help me, the point of these bereavement counsellor meetings was to prepare me for the death of my child and my grief that would set in.

I felt as if everyone were focusing on everything that happens after my child passes away, but why couldn't they have hope instead for my baby? why could not they focus on me and my child now? because my child mattered than and still matters now and he should not have been treated as just something that was going to die.

At that meeting with my bereavement counsellor, I talked to her about clothes and outfits, and would it be possible for me to dress my baby up just as I had always planned.

I was told than that babies with anencephaly born living usually pass away within minutes or hours rather than days, five days usually at the most.

Shopping for baby

After my appointment with my bereavement counsellor, me and mam decided to go on a little shopping trip to take our mind off the bad things and onto the good.

We bought a hospital bag, two, one for the baby and one for me, we also bought three different outfits.

We still thought kaiden was a girl at this point. there was one dress that I admired, it was pink with sparkles on it, and it had tiny little bows on it. The second outfit was a pink floral t-shirt and pink leggings with a matching bib and hat, the last dress was pink also with a tutu skirt which had tiny bunnies on it.

In all the outfits we had to get the size "tiny baby" because we knew my baby was not going to be big.

Even for that little shopping trip I felt normal, for once. It felt like a normal pregnancy, I felt like a mother shopping excitedly for her new-born.

Not knowing what to say to anybody

We told very few people about my babies' condition, not even friends or schoolmates, the only people who knew was the hospital, my family, and my school principal in case something happened during school.

I did not what to say to anyone else." oh my god, you're getting so big, you must be really excited" was a common conversation opener. I would nod and agree and change the subject as fast as I could. Answering by saying "no, I'm not excited, my baby is going to die" never seemed to be the right approach and it's not really the subject you can use to follow up the usual "fine weather we are having today isn't it.

Making memories whilst pregnant

While my mother was doing her weekly shop, I decided to join her, and I am glad I did.
I noticed a scrapbook, the kind where you can put pictures and notes inside of it.
It came to my mind that it would be a brilliant idea to take pictures and capture my pregnancy and special moments that came with it. Moments that I could cherish forever, I decided to buy it because I knew that it would be one of the few things that I would have left of my pregnancy and my child.
We made beautiful memories with my pregnancy and baby.
Me and my nanny went to the cinema to see the new mamma mia film that had just came out, we took selfies, and we kept our cinema tickets and I stuck them in my scrapbook and wrote down the date and how many weeks pregnant I was.
As it was summertime, it was mid-July 2018, it was hot outside. We went to our local beach, which is in bray, we took many photos there and stuck them in my scrapbook.

My goddaughters christening was also in July, there were many more memories made there. Me and my family also went to Los Palmas, in gran Canarias which is one of the Canary Islands off the coast of Spain on holidays, I made memories there to last me a lifetime. About a week before we flew out to los Palmas, I had an appointment with the specialist I was seeing at the coombe hospital. During this check-up it was to see if I could get a copy of my hospital records just in case I went into labour or if any complications arose while I was abroad.

I was told it was very possible to go into pre-term labour, in fact I was told that infants with anencephaly are stillborn in about 75% of cases, so again this is the worry I was carrying on my shoulders every day, every single day not knowing "when" my baby was going to pass away but knowing he was going to die.

He said it would be okay for me to go on holidays, so off we went on our holidays.

On the 25th of July 2018, mine and my baby's bags were packed for los Palmas as a precaution.

Although it was nerve racking, I wanted to enjoy every moment of it and make many memories with my baby, as I knew it would be the only little holiday me and my baby would have with one another, it was an amazing holiday after all , whether it was going to the beach and splashing away or whether it was lying by the poolside in the resort getting a tan or when we went on a long bus journey to Puerto rico and did some shopping or when we went to the exotic animal resort where we see giant lizards, tigers, lions and seen the dolphin show and during that show I got two amazing photos of me and bump kissing a dolphin , those pictures I will cherish forever , I also bought a small pink tiger teddy bear, and at the resort there was a man making bracelets engraving names on them , so I decided to get one made , the girl name I had picked for kaiden when we thought he was a girl was Kaylee.

Thankfully, everything went smooth and me and baby were okay.

That holiday gave me special memories that will remain with me for as long as I live and still to this day my little brothers say to me, "Lauren, I can't believe kaiden was actually in

Spain with us". We continued to take pictures and put them in our scrapbook.

It was the break I needed from constantly being in and out of the hospital, but I still know the worst was still to come.

Telling my siblings, the bad news

As I was due Christmas eve 2018 and that anything could happen to me, my pregnancy, and my baby between august and December so me and my parents only felt it was right to tell my brothers what was wrong with kaiden. Firstly, we told my older brother Jonathan, he was really upset, and he hugged me and told me he was going to help me the best way he can.

Secondly, we told Darragh, the oldest of my younger siblings, if I were to say who was the most excited it would have been him.

I explained to him how sick the baby was and what the outcome would be, but I also explained that he would always be an uncle and that kaiden will always be his nephew and that he will still be able to hold, kiss and meet him.

He just ran and grabbed me and cried, I felt his pain.

Lastly, we told my two younger brothers Daniel and josh who I knew would not really understand.

I explained that their nephew was sick and had to go to heaven because he was too beautiful for this world, but the baby will always be their nephew and as I said to Darragh they will be able to hold, kiss and meet him.

They were upset but also happy that they would still be able to do all those things with him and I also told them if they have any questions, I will always answer them.

As I said before the only people who knew were my close family.

We would give them daily updates on how doctor appointments went and every one of them was so supportive, they would always check up on me and the baby and to make sure I was doing okay.

I am forever thankful to have such a supportive family in my life who have shaped me somehow into the woman I am today.

Every day I carried the burden on my shoulders, knowing that no matter what I did nor what any doctor or specialist did, my baby would die, I would not be able to keep my baby no matter what anyone did. Sometimes I still sit and think to myself, could I have done more? was there anything I could have done to make me and my babies short time together memorable? , I guess this was all just part of the grieving process, but now I know that I did make plenty of memories with my baby that will last me a lifetime , whether it was going to Spain , or even simple things like singing songs to him, they all mean the world and more to me.

Knitting and crocheting hats

From a noticeably young age I always seen my nanny Kelly crocheting and knitting, I was always interested in watching my nanny do it, but I never knew how to knit until I was pregnant.

She had knit my baby a pink and turquoise cardigan, obviously before we found out he was a boy, the turquoise one was my favourite.

As it was summer and it was extremely hot, my pregnant self could not bear to go out to face the heat, so I mostly stayed inside, in the shade. Pregnancy + heat do not mix well together.

Sitting inside all the time was calming and gave me time to reflect and spend time with my baby, but it became boring at times, so one morning I asked my nanny if I could borrow one of her crochet hooks and some wool, my nanny dropped them over later that evening and she showed me the basics.

I wanted to learn how to make baby hats for my own baby as I knew he needed a hat to cover the bandages and gauze that would protect the opening of his head, I watched videos on how to make baby hats online and I learned myself how to do it, I ended up making five hats in total which some of them had crochet flowers and bows attached onto them.

My second bereavement counsellor meeting

About three weeks after we came back from the holiday, I had my second appointment with my bereavement counsellor.

I brought my scrapbook that I made, the hats the I crocheted, the three outfits that I bought, the tiny pink tiger teddy and the baby bracelet that I got made for my baby.

The bereavement counsellor was in awe at what we already had for my baby and how much effort I had put into everything that I showed her, she told me that she was proud of me, to me them words meant the world, it was exactly what I needed to hear.

She proceeded to tell me and my mam that it would be a good idea to start getting everything me and baby needed and to put them in my hospital bags, to have them on the go, in other words she was trying to tell me that time was more than likely running short, and that I was to take each day as it comes.

Getting my hospital bags ready for me and baby

Two days after my meeting with my bereavement counsellor, me, my mama, and nanny went into the city centre in Dublin to get everything me and baby needed for our hospital bags.

Firstly, we went into Primark and bought eight pairs of pyjamas for me, pads for post birth, toiletries, and towels.

We than went into other shops and for baby we bought two more beautiful pink outfits, three bows which were red, white, and pink in colour to go over my babies hats to support them onto his head, frilly socks, blankets, and we also bought pink baby towels in case I got the chance to give my baby a bath and a pack of pink baby sponges to go with it.

We all went to the thunder road café, and we ate dinner and went home and packed all of me and my baby's things into each one of our bags.

And for once that shopping trip was not full of sadness and jealousy of every pregnant woman, I seen shopping excitedly for their healthy new-born, I was excited to meet my new-born as I should have been.

When The doctors assumed, I had polyhydramnios.

On the 1st august, during the middle of the night
woke up with excruciating pains in the bottom of my back, sides, and stomach, I was crying with the pain that I was in.

I was twenty weeks pregnant at this time, I started to think to myself "okay this is it, I'm having my baby" I never experienced such pain in my life.

I was confused, upset and in so much pain. I woke my mam and dad up and they rushed me to the hospital, everybody thought I was in labour, I was rushed into the emergency room as I was high risk already and a foetal medicine patient. The nurses gave me two paracetamol and checked my vitals, after everything was checked one of the doctors examined my cervix, but I was not in labour," if I am not in labour than why am I in so much pain? what is wrong?" is all I could think to myself.

The doctor explained that she thought it was severe Braxton hicks' contractions which are like practice contractions, as it was my first pregnancy, I could not say that it could have not been Braxton hicks because I never felt Braxton hicks' contractions before, but I somehow kept on doubting myself that it was something more serious. the hospital kept me in overnight as a precaution.

This right here was the start of my journey in what felt like endless days and nights in my maternity hospital, I spent nearly most of the rest of my pregnancy in hospital. This is when they told me that my pain could be caused by polyhydramnios, but they never checked.

Getting unexplainably big

On the 27th august, the day before I started back school, I was going into 5th year. I realised not only did none of my jeans fit me suddenly, but my leggings were also getting tight and uncomfortable on me, and my old school bottoms would not have even got a look in.

I had no school uniform for the next day. Me and my mam went to Mothercare to look for maternity trousers even though I was only twenty-four weeks pregnant, I was huge.

 The doctor's told me that I looked as if I was carrying triplets the last time I was in the hospital. We bought maternity trousers in Mothercare, but they had no shirts that fit me in the shop so afterwards we went to Dunnes where I had to buy shirts in a size large out of the men's section when not even all the buttons would close on them.

I did not know why I was getting unexplainably big so fast, I was starting to get pressure in my lower abdomen, it started getting uncomfortable.

Making it to the final Trimester

I never knew how I ever made it to my final trimester. Maybe it was god's plan, or maybe just pure luck, I was so adamant to make it to my final trimester. I was in awe, and so was all the doctors we had encountered on the way. My baby was a true fighter indeed.

I had sixteen weeks left, it started to really hit me, sixteen weeks left of my pregnancy when I knew it would more than likely end much sooner than that.

Blessings from a priest

My nanny Kelly was always really religious, I have faith in God because of my nanny. as a kid me and my nanny always went to a mass ceremony every Saturday evening. My nanny's church group had members from all over the world including one of the priests who had come over from Spain. My nanny talked to the Spanish priest about my situation and the priest wanted t to meet me in person. he came over to my house a week after talking to my nanny and I sat down and spoke to him privately about what I was going through, he gave me words of wisdom and he helped me gain my faith back in God after I was so angry with him.

He asked me for my baby's name, and I told him it was going to be Kaylee Hannah's cooper, he then placed his hand over my head and my baby bump and gave me and my baby a blessing. He told me that my baby had picked me to be her mother and that my baby was lent to me from heaven for a reason, that I had been chosen specially to be her mother. It made me feel so much better, it took a lot of weight off my shoulders, and I gained my faith back with God. I felt like I really needed that blessing at that exact time. I felt important and I felt good enough to be my baby's mother, she chose me to carry her.

Starting my new school year

Even though I was physically ready for school, I had my uniform, books, and copies ready, it did not mean that I was mentally ready.

Before I left for my summer holidays in school the only people who knew was my principle.

I wondered what all the teachers and students would think of me, as they would know that I was pregnant just by looking at my physically pregnant body. I still would have classed myself new to the school, so I have nervous.

It is not as If could have hidden the fact that I was pregnant. Being fifteen and pregnant walking around a school was not normal thing to see.

On the 28th august 2018 I walked into school lifting my head up high but, on the inside, I just wanted the ground to open and swallow me, I wanted to walk down the corridors with my head hung down low, I wanted nobody to notice me, but it was the exact opposite I became the centre of attention, just something to stare at, many of people looked at me deviously whilst they stared at me looking up and down. I just wanted to shout "yeah, so what, I'm fifteen and pregnant, what is it to you?", maybe than people would have looked at something else, anything else.

I just end up brushing it off as I said seeing a fifteen-year-old, noticeably pregnant girl walking around school is not something you would see very often.

I stuck with my small circle of friends for the day.

My last class of the day was geography and one of my friends were sitting beside me, she said "do you see that girl sitting at the back of the class", I replied "yes" whilst I glanced back to get a snippet of her, then my friend told me that the girl in the back was threatening her and slagging her by calling her names at lunchtime. I told my friend not to mind her and we carried on with our classwork.

At the end of that class the girl who was sitting at the back walked toward me and my friend , she started off by saying "if you have a problem say it to my face" whilst looking at me, I replied by saying "I don't have a problem with you , I don't even know you", she than started to give me a devious look, perhaps the most devious look I received that day, she said "yeah, your lucky because if you did I would of kicked that thing out of you ". Right after that sentence I seen black and I just punched her, I could not reprehend what she said nor get over what she said." How dare she say that about my baby, how dare she" is all I could think to myself, "how dare she speak about my sick baby like that and call my baby a thing".

Right after I hit her, some girls ran over and picked her up off the ground by her arms, she ran out of the room, but my teacher ran over to me and brought me downstairs to the office, she repeatedly kept asking me was I okay, but I was completely fine even though I was sitting on the chair with my legs shaking with the anger whilst I was crying. I explained what had happened to my principle and she rang my mam to come pick me up, she insisted that I went to the hospital to get my baby checked, I knew everything was good and that I was not touched or harmed but anyways luckily enough I had my baby's anatomy scan later that evening.

 I even started to think not so soon after what happened that "how was she meant to know my baby was sick?", I had so many emotions go through me.

This girl was a bully but I also I really do not know what got into me that day, I guess it was just my motherly instincts kicking in.

I had never hit anybody before that incident, and I was so shocked that I had done that. Maybe she had tried to pick on me with my friend because I was that "sensitive fifteen-year-old pregnant girl". All I know is that on that day I was a sensitive fifteen-year-old pregnant girl, but I was somewhat stressed, uncomfortable, and extremely hormonal.

The anatomy scan that came with a surprise

On the 29th august I had an anatomy scan which was at 6pm on that day.

Strangely enough, the night before my anatomy scan, I had a dream, a dream where in my scan that was due later that day, I found out I was not having a baby girl but a little baby boy instead.

When I awoke, I told my mother and father about the dream that I had, of course my mother started to laugh whilst saying anxiously "don't you start", as we already had everything, we needed for my baby but it was all in pink and we took the tags off of everything we bought to be able to put them in my hospital bags, there would of been no chance of us being able to return what we had bought. Everything we had was for a girl whether it was between the name we had picked out, clothes, headbands with bows on them even pink towels and sponges.

We later rang my uncle Derek to tell him about the dream that I had, he had always said if I ever had a boy, he would kill me as my uncle only has four daughters and he always longed for a boy. my uncle Derek's fiancé Kiara was also pregnant at this time with their fourth daughter, and he was only delighted when we told him I was having a girl because if he did not have a boy, I was not allowed unless I called him "Derek" after him. My uncles only response was "get the boat "whilst giggling about it.

Me and my mother left our home at 5.30pm, we still could not stop smiling and reminiscing about the dream that I had, we laughed about if it did happen at the scan that we would have to get everything all over again for my "baby boom" as I called my bump.

It was only a dream at the end of the day, me and my mam stopped messing because I started to get quite stressed about it, I started to focus on my baby's health, that maybe another problem had arisen…. Which it did. As I was lying in the bed at the hospital, I asked the specialist doctor could my mother record the ultrasound which he agreed to as me and the specialist did not know when was going to be the last time, I get to see my baby moving around.

As my mother started recording the specialist looked confused and he let out a giggle. What in the world was he laughing at? I thought to myself, is he laughing at my baby? I did not know why I thought that it was nonsense, it would have been totally unprofessional. He turned around and looked at me with a grin on his face, he said "I think I made a mistake" as he let out another giggle, "it's a boy" he said extatically, I was shocked, I was happy. Me and my mam just looked at each other and could not stop laughing, I did not know whether to laugh or cry, I did not know whether it was a nervous or a happy laugh. My mam said to the specialist "are you sure", the specialist laughed as he moved the arrow on the screen to in between my baby's legs. I started to laugh nervously "he's definitely a boy ", I said.

The conversation began to become serious, my sons omphalocele had grown bigger and no improvements whatsoever with my baby's head or health in general. I did not think anything would have improved, my baby was "incompatible with life", but after all I found out

I did not have a daughter, but I had a little boy instead, a son and that little boy meant and still does mean the world to me.

Then suddenly, the specialist asks my mam to politely switch the video off on her phone, "what could be wrong now?" I said to myself, even though I knew my son was sick or "terminally ill", I began to get that feeling, the emotionless, worrying feeling, I felt dizzy. "What could it possibly be now?".

He noticed that something was wrong with my babies heart, but he did not give any diagnosis for a condition , he began to explain that the omphalocele that held his liver and bowel in vitro (outside of body) may have pulled his heart slightly but his heart was still beating , that's all that mattered to me , his beautiful heart was still beating inside of me, he was still jumping and leaping inside of my womb and his kicks and thumps were getting stronger and stronger as he got that bit bigger, he was so energetic but he was still very sick , I wondered how that little boy , that baby jumping around on that screen that I was looking at was so poorly.

The specialist noticed something else, I had way too much amniotic fluid, a "abnormal" amount of fluid was the way the specialist worded it. I had well over twice the average amount of amniotic fluid that a "normal" pregnancy would have, the condition I was diagnosed with on that day was polyhydramnios, it is a medical condition describing an excess amount of amniotic fluid in the amniotic sac and it is only seen in around 1% of pregnancies, it is typically diagnosed when the amniotic fluid index (AFI) is greater than 24cm. Being diagnosed with polyhydramnios led to the chances of more complications to be increased such as the following,

- Preterm labour/contractions
- Preterm rupture of membranes
- Foetal malposition
- Maternal respiratory compromise
- Umbilical cord prolapses.
- Uterine atony
- Abruptio placentae

"What else could go wrong" is all I could say to myself, I felt as though everything that could go wrong was happening to me.
I asked was there any cure or method that could reduce the fluid, he told me that there is a method that was called amnio drainage

, during amnio drainage they use a general anaesthetic to numb a certain part of the stomach and put a long needle and tube through your stomach and into the womb and they drain the liquid through the tube Into a large machine, during the procedure they do an ultrasound also whilst looking at the baby to make sure the baby does no go near the needle or the tube, he explained that this is a risky procedure as it can cause rupture of membranes and or preterm labour, I learned soon after that , that polyhydramnios is usually connected with anencephaly (my babies neural tube defect).

Anencephaly only occurs in an estimated 1-1000 pregnancies, but most of those pregnancies end in early miscarriage and in only 1-10,000 babies in the United States are born with anencephaly and 75% of those babies would be delivered sleeping (stillborn).

Anencephaly mostly occurs in female foetuses whilst my baby was a boy. everything my baby was diagnosed with was fatal and rare, how could he be so sick and still fighting? for a baby so small. I knew in that moment my baby boy was a fighter, he fought to survive, and he fought to be on earth with his mam. I chose the perfect name for him "kaiden", meaning warrior in Gaelic, and what a warrior he was.

The specialist continued to tell me that the procure did come with risks, but it was the right option for me. It was not a one-time off procedure, I had to keep on getting them done once the amniotic fluid kept growing back right up until I gave birth to my son. As the fluid grew, I felt uncomfortable with sleeping, walking even breathing became a daily struggle, it also gave me terrible heartburn.

It seemed to me the best option, my only option.

During that scan when I got diagnosed, he measured the exact amount of amniotic fluid in was carrying and told me he wanted to see me in two weeks' time to compare the levels of amniotic fluid and to see the rate it was increasing. Me and my mam both agreed that it would be a great idea. I got a few 4D photos of him that day, I could see his button nose, his hands a foot, his lips, I could see everything so clearly, it was hard to believe that he was mine. His cheeks were the chubbiest cheeks I had ever seen. I could not wait to surprise my family that my baby was not a girl but a beautiful baby boy instead. My dad was thrilled that he was having a grandson, my four brothers could not have been happier, but it was safe to say my uncle Derek nearly hung up the phone when I told him.

Shopping all over again

I was twenty-four weeks pregnant; I was told that I was lucky to have made it that far, I caried him to the third trimester. It was believed that I did not have that much time left, I was dreading for that time to come, I did not have that much time left and I had absolutely nothing for my baby ever since I found out he was a boy.

Two days after we were told I was having a son me, my mam and my nanny went shopping AGAIN, we went to Mothercare to pick up some boy outfits. We got into Mothercare and went over to the baby boy section, I admired everything, and I could not pick favourites and in that moment, I broke down inside, I wanted to buy nearly everything I seen, how I wished my son could wear all those clothes, if I were lucky, I would be able to dress him in at most four outfits. The cots, Moses baskets, prams, seeing all of them broke my heart, I knew that I would never see my baby in any of those things.

I picked up a few beautiful outfits, one being a little blue teddy bear dungaree set that came with a vest, I got a tractor and car set with matching bibs, I also got a set which had moons and stars on it, it was trousers and a t-shirt which had "mummy's star and daddy's son".

Soon after that we went to Tesco and bought the cutest packet of little socks, blue baby sponges and towels, we also got two more perfect little outfits, one of them was a grey lion outfit which had little paws on the hands and feet and eyes and ears and a lion mane on the hat that came with it. The second outfit I got in Tesco was a navy dinosaur outfit with spikes on the back of the baby grow on the hat there was eyes and sharp teeth, as soon as I seen that outfit I said to my mam "ma imagine he was born on Halloween, I would have to put him in that dinosaur outfit".

We went to Dunnes stores after and we bought three soft blue blankets, one with white clouds on it. We brought all the things home and emptied all the things I bought for a girl out of my hospital bag and put them into a plastic bag until we figured out what we wanted to do with them.

I decided it would be good, generous, and just if I donated all the premature girl clothes, blankets and new towels and sponges to the coombe hospital for all the premature babies. I kept the bracelet I got made in Spain for my baby as a keepsake.
I was advised to get premature clothes for kaiden as we did not know when he was going to be born and even, so he was going to be a small baby.

Donating the premature clothes

The following day after I went shopping, I had a meeting with the bereavement counsellor, I brought in the bag full of premature baby girl clothes, cardigans, and the hats I crocheted. it was all worth it when I see the smile on her face. I was so happy to help the premature babies that may have needed them. The bereavement counsellor was in awe, she fell in love with all the dresses and bows but mostly the pink tiger teddy that I bought whilst on my holiday in Spain. She went on to saying that many mothers in need will receive all the beautiful outfits, this made me smile, I was going to help mothers in need.

Then I got asked the question no mother should ever been asked, she asked me did I have any funeral, burial, or cremation plans. I did not know what to say or how to even begin thinking about answering that question. I knew I would need to decide with what to do with my babies' body whether I did it before or after birth, I needed to think about if an autopsy was necessary, did I prefer a full funeral, a memorial service, funeral prayers, a private graveside service, or no service at all? Embalming? Burial or cremation? what kind of casket or urn? burial in a cemetery? scatter ashes or keep them? I just did not know how to process that question, all those things, why did I have to decide what to do with my babies' body? all I wanted to do was keep him, that is all I wanted. I started to cry during that meeting, I knew she did not mean it in any harm, it was her job at the end of the day, and she was right, no matter how much I did not want to, I needed to make the decision.

Preliminary funeral and burial planning

After an emotional meeting, me, my mama, and dad sat down and decided that we would talk about our options, I knew I wanted to bury him, but why should I have even had to think about burying my own child? no mother should have to think about burying or cremating their own baby.

I still believed that a miracle could happen, but I did begin to lose hope. I started to research local cemeteries where my son, who was not even born yet was going to be buried. I thought about new lands cross cemetery, but I soon found out that bohernabreena cemetery which was five minutes away from me had an "angel plot" where was a certain plot in the cemetery where only babies were buried, I thought that it would be so nice for kaiden to be buried where all other babies were buried, he would be with all the other babies. We drove up to bohernabreena that evening to make our final decision and as soon as we drove into the cemetery it was evident where the angel plot was, the solar lights not only lit up the sky, but they lit up my heart also. There were many lights that lit up the whole cemetery.

I held my bump and cried, even though it was beautiful I did not want my baby there, I wanted him with me. God works in mysterious ways, but why did he pick me? Why was this cemetery my baby's faith? Why was this the path that I was going to take in life? And why was that going to be the only place where I would be able to visit my own baby? So many questions that would be left unanswered. I made the tough but right decision that it would be the perfect place to lay my son to rest.

There is nothing I could do to spare my son of his faith, not any doctor, specialist or surgeon could either. My baby's faith was always in the hands of God, the same way as all of us. As I always said God had other plans for my son, I just wished that the plans included me.

As we drove out of the cemetery to go home, my heart felt heavy and my eyes filled up with tears, I held my bump and looked to the sky, I could see clouds, clouds shaped as elephants, was this a sign? I got home and my nanny surprised me with a blue elephant baby comforter, it was hardly just coincidence, in that moment I knew then and there that they were little signs from my angels.

My first amnio drainage

It was the day where I had to go to the maternity hospital to determine whether I needed an amnio drainage. Of course, I was nervous, who wouldn't be? I was scared, scared of all the risks that accompanied it, scared of rupturing membranes and going into labour, meeting my baby too soon, I needed to spend more time with him, I did not want it to happen yet, and I was afraid of how bad the procedure would hurt. I remember the night before my appointment I went onto YouTube and searched videos of the procedure getting done, I do not know why I did that because that is what made me ten time more nervous when I thought it would prepare me.

I had a fear of needles and even the thoughts of a large needle going into my womb scared the life out of me.

We went into the specialist for an ultrasound and the scan did indeed show that the amount of amniotic fluid in my womb was increasing even more than the specialist thought it would, he insisted that I got the amnio drainage on that day as he was free that evening. I started to get anxious and nervous, he said that he could get me admitted into the hospital right away because I would need to stay in the hospital for twenty-four hours after the procedure just to keep an eye on me in case anything did go wrong. Even though I was afraid to get the procedure done the specialist told me that I would not feel any pain, just discomfort as they give me a local anaesthetic and right after the amnio drainage my stomach would feel much lighter, that there would not be as much pressure and I would not get heartburn as much, it would be easier for me to breath.

I agreed to get the procedure done later that day.

Me and my mother were escorted to the fourth floor of the maternity hospital, St. Gerard's ward, this was the ward where women would stay if they got surgery for example a hysterectomy, or where women would say if they miscarried or had a stillbirth or for types of women like me, a foetal medicine patient.

I got my very own room that came with my own bathroom and shower.

My mam had to stay overnight with me, as I was under the age of eighteen.

Me and my mam got settled into the room whilst my father got all the hospital bags and got in the car to drop them up to the hospital including kaidens bag, just as a precaution in case anything did go wrong. My dad bought McDonalds for the three of us to cheer up my mood and to calm my nerves.

At around 6am that evening, the midwife came In and told us that the specialist was ready to do the procedure, the midwife escorted me and my mam down to the second floor of the maternity hospital to the specialist's room and we waited for about five minutes for him to call us in.

I laid down onto the bed while my mam sat on a chair beside the bed in which I was laying on.

The specialist's assistant situated herself in the room also, she was there for all the procedures and appointments I had from then, onwards.

Firstly, the specialist got everything ready on the table such as the needle and tubing and the vacuum machine that would suction the amniotic fluid.

The assistant nurse proceeded to apply the cold ultrasound jelly on my stomach and started the ultrasound to figure out where my baby was lying to determine where to pierce the needle.

The specialist prepped my stomach with iodine, tis an antiseptic which gave my skin a yellow tint, he then placed surgical blue tach cloth over my stomach and the side of my face so I would not see what was happening which I think helped a lot in that situation because I probably would have freaked out, I just focused looking at my baby boy on the screen, I just focused on him.

Just before the procedure started, the specialist asked me if I would agree for him to take a sample of the amniotic fluid, a "amniocentesis" to send over to England because as he said before, when a baby has anencephaly and an omphalocele it is usually ruled out that the baby has Edward syndrome or something else that was chromosomally wrong.

My mother signed the form for the amniocentesis as we thought it would bring me closure for my baby's condition.

He then proceeded to make sure my baby was not jumping around, he then gave me a local anaesthetic to numb a part of my stomach, he then placed the needle in slowly, it did not hurt although it was very discomforting. Once he got to my womb with the needle and tubing, I felt an immense pressure and what felt like a pop. It was a twenty-gauge needle that the specialist used. he got a syringe and suctioned a small amount of amniotic fluid which contains foetal tissue, they can also use this small amount of fluid to determine the sex of the baby, we just hoped that he was a boy after donating everything I had for a girl.

My baby clearly got frightened by the needle and he decided that he would topple to one side of my stomach, this was the weirdest feeling I ever got, I never felt my baby move that strongly.

After the amniocentesis was complete, the specialist attached the tubing to a vacuum assisted device with vacuum bottles and he then started to drain the amniotic fluid, the number one thing I remembered from the procedure.

Was the horrific smell, it reeked of urine and I soon found out after that, amniotic fluid is partially made up of baby urine as the baby swallows the amniotic fluid and urinate it back out in the womb, the specialist explained that the reason many women carrying babies with anencephaly develop polyhydramnios is because babies with anencephaly have very weak swallowing reflexes, this means the baby is not really swallowing much which leads to the build-up of amniotic fluid.

As the specialist continued to drain my amniotic fluid from my womb, the stench still began to linger across the room. The specialist and his assistant constantly kept tabs on my baby's activity, it got to a certain stage where my baby was so active and curious about what was going on that I could see his hand reaching out and trying to grasp the tubing. the specialist and I got anxious about if the tubing prodded his toes or hands, the doctor decided that he had drained enough amniotic fluid and he then took the tubing out of my womb. he put more amniotic fluid on the area where he pierced my skin, he put gauze and a bandage also.

He set up another appointment for three weeks following my procedure and he wrote a prescription for the midwives to keep me dosed up on tylex as I would be in some pain and discomfort from the procedure.
The assistant nurse brought me a wheelchair and wheeled me back to my room on the fourth floor.

Post procedure

I was in disbelief at how much my little boy had grown in just such a short amount of time, it is true when they say, "they grow so fast". His long legs and arms, I could not believe it. that was most definitely one of many of my "proud mammy" moments.

The staff in the coombe hospital in which I attended were amazing, they truly did all that they could for me and my son and there are not enough thanks in the world for all they have done.

I laid in the hospital bed in my room whilst my mam kept our family up to date about how the procedure went.

I was than given my first dose of tylex, I got in for a nice warm shower, I washed my hair, and my mam gave me special treatment and dried my hair for me whilst I had no energy, the hospital caterers than brought me in a sandwich.

I did not realise how much discomfort I was enduring before only until I got the amnio drainage, I fell fast asleep comfortably even on a hospital bed.

I was only awoken once during the night by the midwife that was on night duty to give me my second dose of tylex, I got up out of my bed and I went to the bathroom, the midwife held me and helped me to walk to the bathroom. I was confused as to why she was holding me; I was perfectly capable of doing it on my own, she explained that the tylex tablets can sometimes make people feel dizzy and weak, she waited outside the bathroom for me and helped me walk back to my bed. She took great care of me, I got in to bed and fell back asleep.

The morning came and I was awoken by the caterers for breakfast in bed, boiled egg, and toast.

The doctor that was on call, did his rounds on the ward that I was on, which again was St. Gerard's ward. he came into my room and introduced himself, he asked me how I was feeling after the procedure such as pain and discomfort, I told him I felt the procedure went very well and the tylex worked well for the pain, I also told him I had a great sleep, which I had not had in quite some time, I was feeling much better.

He said he thinks it would be fine for me to go home since I was feeling much better. Me and my mam packed up all our things and my dad picked us up from the maternity hospital.

My bump looked much smaller compared to the size that it had been, it was so strange to be able to walk and breath in comfort.

During the next few days after the surgery, I was feeling so much more movement from my little boy and I could see him pressing out his little hands, I would tap my bump and he would kick it back with his little toes, one of my "proud mammy moments also.

I felt so blessed and privileged to have had them little moments but huge memories with my son.

Whenever I tried to let my mam or dad feel his kicks or whenever I tried to take a video of his movements, he would make a mockery out of me, he was a funny little devil for that.

Whilst I was feeling all these new and amazing movements from my little boy, I found a poem online that I read every day and I would love to share it with all my readers.

This poem brings me back to such happy memories and moments that I spent with my baby boy.

I love you little baby.
you are such a part of me.
I cannot wait to hold you in my arms.
And hug you tenderly.
No matter what you look like
You are beautiful my love.
A precious gift bequeathed to me.
From heaven up above
Each time I feel you moving.
My heart is filled with joy.
I think that very soon.
I will hold you my little boy.
I am counting ever moment.
Till your mine at last, my sweet
It will not be long until your birth.
Then finally we will meet.

that poem is beautifully written by an
anonymous poet, I believe it is the sweetest
poem that does not bring me sadness, but
happiness, it brings me back to the time I
spent with my baby.

Telling the world my story

I was stunned by the anencephaly groups I had joined on Facebook; everybody was sharing their story and it encouraged me to share mine. I picked up the courage and I made my own Facebook group and I started to share my story and my journey as we went through it.

People from all over the world joined my Facebook group and was shocked by such a journey we had already been on.

Everybody watched in awe as my journey continued.

It was important to me to share me and my baby's story, my baby was not just going to be another statistic.

I met this girl online that lived in England, she had previously lost a baby and I stayed in contact with her throughout my journey. When I found out I was having a baby boy she sent me over a beautiful blue blanket with stars on it with his name embroidered onto it.

I never felt such kindness from a stranger.

New strange cravings

Around this time in my pregnancy, I started to experience even more cravings, iceberg lettuce dipped in Nutella, I craved the smell of nail varnish remover which I stayed away from and mashed potato which I had never eaten before I was pregnant.

These cravings were weird and strange to me.

Starting to shut myself down.

I started to shut myself down. I became depressed and anxious. I was not looking after myself the way I should have been. I became so lost and drowning myself in my thoughts knowing that my baby was going to die and there was nothing I could do about it, there was nothing I, or any other doctor in the world could do to save him.

It felt as if I was sinking into a black hole. My baby was given a death sentence from the second he was conceived and there was nothing I could do about it. I felt that me and my family were so focused on preparing we and my baby for his death instead of embracing his life which was totally untrue, this, accompanied with the fact that I could not save my own son made me feel like the worst mother in the world.

Nothing in this world can prepare you for the pain of losing your child or knowing that they are going to die.

"Incompatible with life", it was written on all my documents. If he were inside of me, he could live, supported by my body but as soon as he was born, and his little body had to take over he would die.

I just wanted to feel normal, I wanted to embrace my pregnancy like everybody else. I wanted to have a normal pregnancy, but the thing was I did not have a normal pregnancy and that was just something that I had to except.

I went through the rest of my pregnancy hoping for that one in a million chance that the doctors were wrong.

I could feel my son moving and I could feel him grow stronger every day.

I wanted to believe that the doctors were wrong and that miracles could happen, but in what world would I get that miracle.

I also felt completely different than the woman that stood next to me in Tesco, still waiting for me to answer her question. we were both pregnant, both looking at impossibly tiny new-born outfits, both of us trying to decide whether we should get the matching socks and hats. "I cannot wait to dress him in that too", she said to me, "is that the outfit you're going to bring him home in", I felt like punching her in the face, I felt like breaking down all I could do was fake it by saying "yes, it's the cutest little outfit, I was thinking of bringing him home in that outfit".

Anticipatory grief

Sometimes I wondered whether grieving before my baby died was normal, it made me feel even more guilty.

Naturally, people grieve after a loved one dies but even before death when you know that death is probable or imminent, I learned that it was normal to start grieving even before my baby died, it is called anticipatory grief and it continued throughout my pregnancy and my baby's short life.

Anticipatory grief, this is what I felt guilty of experiencing during my pregnancy and I could not help feeling that way. I felt as if I should have been focusing on my baby's life but all I could focus on was my baby's death.

I did learn during my pregnancy that anticipatory grief can have psychologically positive aspects. For instance, knowing that my baby will die enhanced my appreciation of my baby and the time that I had left, it sharpened my focus and helped order my priorities, it pressed me to attune to my baby and to be mindfully present during precious moments I had with my little boy.

Another positive aspect of anticipatory grief was that I experienced a more gentle, gradual goodbye instead of having to meet death suddenly and let go of my baby.

I began to grieve while I still had my baby's presence.

I adjusted to the prospect of letting go, I knew I still got to hold my baby close.

I was told by the bereavement counsellor that when I am letting go must begin in earnest after death, that recalling these memories of holding my baby close physically and mentally can help me continue to adjust.

I remember during my pregnancy, many times I could not sleep, and I would just go sit and cry. During those moments he would always kick me, it was always that reminder that he was still there, and I should not be so sad yet.

An overview of my grieving process

Anticipatory grief was an early and integral part of my grieving process, which occupied a significant portion of my emotional energy for many months. grief is so agonizing which is why many people believe that grieving is something bad, to be avoided or something to be gotten over as quick as possible. Grieving whether before or after birth is a painful but necessary process. It enabled me to come to terms with loss and to move forward in spite of it. Grieving is ultimately a constructive process whereby you gradually let go of what might have been and what is. In general, the deeper the investment in what might have been, the deeper the grief. Even before the diagnosis I was already invested in my baby. According to research and personal experience bereaved parents commonly report that their baby's death was the most significant grief that they have ever experienced.

I figured out that understanding the grieving process did not spare me from its ravages, but when my emotions made sense, it made it easier for me to cope.

Instead of drowning in a seemingly endless sea of pain, I   remembered that grieving is a natural and important process.

Instead of trashing aimlessly and exhausting, I could identify my emotions and move through them toward solid ground, I also moved toward safe harbour by expressing my grief through purposeful action that honoured my baby's life.

Informed about grief, what I was grieving and how I grieved, I responded constructively instead of destructively, with intelligence rather than desperation.

More important, during my pregnancy, understanding grief motivated me to be present with my baby and I gathered memories and keepsakes that carried me toward healing even beyond the end of my baby's life.

The start of my endless, sleepless nights in hospital

On Saturday 8th of September, I woke up in the middle of the night with sharp shooting pains and lots of pressure in my back and pelvic area, it felt as if I was having those Braxton hicks' contractions but nearly ten times more painful. I was twenty-five weeks pregnant, and it had only been one week after my amnio drainage.

I woke my mam and dad up and she and my dad got up as quick as they could in a panic. I still was not mentally or physically prepared to have my baby, these pains felt much worse from the ones before. My mam grabbed her bag along with mine and my baby's, we got into the car and my dad drove me to the hospital as fast as he could. We were rushed straight to the emergency room, where they examined me, but I was not dilated which meant I was not in labour, I started to wonder whether the volume of amniotic fluid had increased rapidly over that two weeklong period, but it had only been two weeks. The pain continued to grow stronger, and it started to become really Intense, so the specialist strongly advised that I stayed overnight to keep a close eye on me which I agreed to. The specialist's assistant escorted us down to the same room I stayed in when I got my first amnio drainage on St. Gerard's ward.

The doctor soon came into the room and felt it was important to do an ultrasound on my stomach to see how my baby was coping. The doctor finished up doing the ultrasound and he explained that he believed that my pain was coming from the growing amount of amniotic fluid in my room, it made my womb contract. He said that yes, the amniotic fluid in my womb was increasing but there was not enough amniotic fluid for him to do an amnio drainage procedure.

After the doctor left, my mam went over to the shop across from the maternity hospital and got us both a subway whilst I got in for a hot shower to try numbing the pain. I ate my subway roll and I felt so nauseous that I vomited up my roll, I could not keep anything down my stomach, it was tiring and torturing. why did my pregnancy have to be the way it was?, I have to admit , yes it was very difficult, draining and tiring enduring such a tough pregnancy at fifteen years old but I never , not even once questioned the choice that I made to carry my baby to term even though he was "incompatible with life", yes I knew he was going to die , and yes I went through a traumatic and painful both mental and physical pregnancy but the best part of it all was getting to hold my babies hands , grasping him closer to my chest , kissing his soft and gentle cheeks and grabbing onto his body whether warm or cold . In them moments time stood still and, in those moments, not one other thing mattered to me and in those moments everything that I had been through and everything that I had endured was all worth it.

Soon after I got sick the midwife came into my room and gave me my first dose of tylex and checked my vitals and checked my baby's heartbeat which was perfectly fine. I than attempted to go asleep, I was twisting and turning all throughout the night.

The next morning, I woke up after a horrible night's sleep, still in utter pain.

I ate my breakfast and I got sick right after that too.

The doctor on call did his rounds around the fourth floor of the hospital and came into my room, I had to tell him the truth that I was still in tremendous pain. He explained that there was nothing him or the hospital could do for me other than to help me manage the pain that I was in as there was not enough fluid to be able to do the amnio drainage procedure and I was not in labour. He wanted to keep me in for that night also.

Not long after the doctor left, the midwife came in and checked my vitals as well as my baby's heart rate, all was doing fine except for the pain that I was in, the midwife gave me a second dose of tylex. I had to be given two tylex every six hours, I was also given an anti-nausea tablet along with the tylex to stop me from getting sick. I was able to eat my hospital dinner without getting sick which was a start. I was given two more tylex accompanied with a anti nauseous tablet and I fell asleep, with much less difficulty than the night before, I felt so much better. the doctor came around the next morning and told me he felt as if I was capable of being able to go home, my mum

discharged me from the hospital as I was underage, and we went home. I was given a prescription for tylex to take twice a day whilst I was at home, to keep me comfortable.
They sent me a letter to come in for a physio appointment, which helped. I got a supportive belt which I wrapped around the bottom of my stomach to help relieve the pressure, I had to wear it every day.

Layers of loss and grief

My grief had many layers, as I gradually realized everything that I was losing. I was losing the chance to raise my child, I also grieved for the milestones I would miss- the first tooth, the first step, the first day of school. I was losing what could have been experienced together, such as sharing my favourite stories, playing at the beach, or camping in the woods. These losses were real.

He will never be able to have the life that we all have been able to experience. All of the images I had in my mind I knew would never come true. I will never see my baby walk or talk and this list goes on.

Realizing the broken dreams was one of the hardest things I had to face.

I cried and I cried, and I cried. I cried for the loss of life, the utter waste, the utter shame, and utter loss of potential. I could have had a son. He could have been amazing. I would have given him an amazing life, loved him beyond love. He would have had an amazing life, with me.

There were also many related losses I was acutely experiencing. For example, I grieved for my dreams of a blissful pregnancy, a joyous birth, a healthy new-born, and an uncomplicated homecoming.

I felt like I was cheated out of a happy pregnancy.

All of these losses were mixed unto my mourning.

Moving through grief

By moving through my grief, I freed myself to experience the joy of my baby's life. While this may sound contradictory, it rests on the fact that emotional repression is not selective: if I repressed my painful emotions, I suppressed my pleasurable moments as well. So, if I avoided grief, I would have ended up avoiding joy as well. This was a high price I had to pay, particularly while my baby was alive.

When I was in the midst of grief, it was difficult to believe that the hard work of moving through that pain lead to joy or healing. Grief was distressing-even frightening- in its power but making sense of the turmoil helped me to tolerate it.

Grief encompasses many emotional and physical feelings.

I experienced shock, disorientation, irritability, guilt, failure, sorrow, withdrawal, hopelessness, anxiety, and yearning. I also experienced array of physical symptoms, including fatigue, tightness in my throat and chest, and changes in my appetite and sleep. Everybody's expression of grief is as unique as they are.

Any emotion in the dictionary probably applied to me: anger, confusion, denial, fear, sadness, love for my baby, tremendous fear of the unknown and deep sadness over the loss of the healthy baby I had dreamed of .... The list goes on and on.

Grief can be chaotic, and there are no timetables or deadlines. It is never a neat set of stages, but a fluid mix of feelings. I experienced ups and downs, periods of despair and periods of respite. I cycled through feelings many times over. Progress would be one step forward and two steps back. Still, I strengthened my adjustment and making an overall movement toward renewed purpose. But I knew that it was ok to feel caught up in a process that was beyond my control.

I had a desire to celebrate my baby's life and give him as much love as possible in what little time I had, and back to sadness that I knew I would not have my baby for very long. It is truly amazing how many tears a person can generate. Just when I thought that I had cried about as much as I could, more tears came.

Sometimes I wondered if I was dealing with it okay. Many times, people would say, in giving me a compliment, that they could not believe how positive I was about it. Then, I would wonder, am I going nuts?

I knew it was okay to cry in front of people, but I could not cry all day long, so I kept my tears inside and would let them all out while alone. My shower became my safe place to cry. This happened sometimes uncontrollably; I was alone with my thoughts, and I often succumbed to tears.

Grief evolves over time. while grief was generally chaotic, I also felt a sense of progress as my emotions evolved. I felt myself adjusting to my situation and thinking, "okay, now what?" and as I settled into my pregnancy, I came to realise that I wanted to be able to see past my pain and also experience positive moments with my baby.

Evolving emotions

As my emotions evolved throughout my pregnancy, there was a natural progression from shock and disbelief toward facing reality, coping with it, adjusting to it, and moving forward with it. This allowed me to gradually face and cope with what I could handle without overwhelming myself. As I moved my energy from fighting reality to accepting it, I figured out ways to move forward in the face of it. I embraced the rhythm of my special pregnancy and found myself captivated by the wonder of that special life.

I felt inspired to fill my baby's life with love, eager to welcome my baby into my arms, and determined to help my baby die a dignified natural death. I made a concerted effort to reap as many positives as I could for as long as my baby was with me.

The following sections address some of the evolving emotions I faced, including the following:

- Shock, numbness, and denial
- Conflicting thoughts and feelings
- Guilt, failure, and anger

Shock, numbness, and denial

Since learning about my baby's condition, I had moments where I was not feeling much of anything. I found it hard to believe that I was even in this position, and I questioned whether the prognosis was as grim as the tests indicated. I found it difficult to absorb the shocking news and to come to grips with all that my baby's diagnosis – and my pregnancy- entails. I felt like I spent periods of time in a daze.

I think I became numb for the rest of the pregnancy. I did not know how to cope. I wanted so badly to enjoy my pregnancy and talk about the little experiences I had, but I felt like I was not supposed to talk about it.

I knew my baby was going to die, every kick was a painful reminder that his life would not be.

The pain was so great, the anger was great, and the disbelief was great. Getting out of bed was a struggle. it took me a long time to realize that I was carrying a baby who needed me. I did not feel worthy of maternity clothing for about a month until my size gave me no choice.

Conflicting thoughts and feelings

As my numbness and shock wore off, I began to feel the force of my grief. But my grief was not straightforward. Because I was facing this incomprehensible fusion of new life and impending death, I expected to experience wild swings of joy and sorrow, celebration, and dread.

As I prepared to welcome, I also prepared to let go. Vacillation is the nature of anticipatory grief and was a normal part of continuing my pregnancy. Many parents swing back and forth between conflicting emotions and thoughts.

Every emotion that their it would course through my body on a daily basis. Even good things like kicks would eventually lead to sadness. Would that be the last time I ever felt him move?

I did have a few times that I thought things would be better if kaiden would just come already! The daily anticipation was wearing. I wished that we could just start to move on, and yet I knew I wanted to cherish each day I had to feel him move, kick, punch, and just be.

Some days I was overcome with a mother love for him, protective and nurturing. other days, I tried hard not to think about him, to not think of losing him.

When I was still pregnant all I could think about was that I knew I should treasure this life, treasure the bulge of my abdomen, knowing that life still existed inside of media knew I should cherish ever kick, knowing that this is the relationship that I would have with this little one. But why did I purposely fall in love knowing the pain increases when love is present?

I was struggling to see the good that could of came out of a life so short.

I did not want to be sad all the time. I needed to laugh, I needed to be able to just be "normal".

It was not that I was not showing strength; it was that I knew I would have plenty of time to cry, back than was not the time.

It helped to remind myself that whatever my mix of feelings, that mix was what was right for me. It was part of my process of coming to terms with my pregnancy and my baby's condition. as long as I felt like I was in touch with my grief and moving through it, however slowly, I was continuing to adjust.

Guilt, failure, and anger

Feelings of guilt, failure and anger arose from the belief that I had control over what happens to me.

No one has complete control over their reproductive fortunes, but at first, I protested this reality. Anger was a way to lash out at the unfairness of my twist of fate; guilt and failure stemmed from my feelings of responsibility. Even if I recognised that I did not have complete control, it was normal to feel responsible for my baby's condition or to worry that I may be seen that way. After all, I reasoned, this child was conceived by me and carried by me. I wondered if there were aspects of my genetic makeup, medical history, or lifestyle that contributed to my baby's condition. I felt responsible for disappointing those close to me who were eagerly anticipating my baby's arrival. I knew my baby's condition was due to random chance, but I still felt some sense of responsibility and attendant feelings of guilt and failure.

I was frightened that I had done something to make my baby sick, even though I knew I had done everything right and everything I was supposed to.

I felt terrible guilt—I should have been able to save him. I was letting everyone in my family down by not being able to protect him and bring him safely into this world.

I was more worried about my parents. I wanted to be strong for them and let them think I was okay, even if I was not. Who wants their parents to worry about them?

Anger is a natural reaction to feeling like your life is spinning out of control. I felt angry at the situation, my body, fate, mother nature and God. I was irritable and felt angry at people for not knowing how to support me. I felt incensed at parents who took fertility for granted or who neglected their children.

I struggled with the unfairness of this; I wanted this baby. All I wanted was a child to love, to raise, to be a part of the family that I had always dreamed of having.

Some days I was angry at everything.

All of these feelings I were experiencing are common and natural aspects of grief, part of my process of coming to terms with the injustice of my situation. The key was not to get stuck in destructive self-recrimination. It helped me to remember the following.

- Sometimes bad things happen to good people.
- My baby's condition was not a punishment that I deserved; it was a fluke of nature and a tragic, unexpected detour.
- I did not knowingly cause or choose this fate of my child.
- Feeling guilty is not the same as being guilty.

Feeling a sense of failure is not the same as being a failure.

It also helped to remember that part of coming to terms with my baby's condition was to realize that I cannot control every aspect of my life. this realization helped me to take charge of what I can control.

I did everything possible to be a good mom. that was one of the hardest things for me, was losing control.

If I were in control, I would have a healthy baby boy. but once I found out that he was not going to live, I thought, I would just make the most out of what I could do.

Confronting fears

I always feared the next step. When I first received the diagnosis, I was not afraid of the coming weeks. When I only had a few more weeks to go, I worried about labour complications. I was afraid of giving birth, not because of the pain. I wanted to stay pregnant forever because kaiden would be alive.

Fear arose from many sources. I had many worries about how everything would unfold. I worried about physical and emotional suffering for my baby, for myself, and for my family members. I feared the process of childbirth and I was afraid of what my baby would look like. I was afraid of my baby's death and my fears and worries seemed endless.

I was afraid of the grief, of never being able to move on.

Fears of the unknown

Continuing my pregnancy naturally posed many unknowns that caused anxiety. I did not know anyone who had done this before me, I did not find the reassurances I needed in the typical pregnancy guidebooks. This journey, many of mothers have been through is largely uncharted. how long will my pregnancy last? What kind of labour and birth should I be expecting? Will my baby be born alive? What will happen after my baby's birth? all these questions I had whilst pregnant were left unanswered, answers unknown. My caregivers had noticeably little experience with babies like mine, and the predictions were merely educated guesses.

The worst part was not knowing what would happen. I was preoccupied with trying to know what would happen to kaiden.; would he die at birth? How would I cope with what he might look like?

Every day I wondered if it was going to be "the day". I had read that it was typical for babies with kaidens condition to be born from 20 weeks to 40 weeks. I was able to cope by enjoying the life I felt inside of me, but that did not mean I was not full of anxiety every day. It was by far the most difficult thing I have ever done and probably will do.

I did not know when the baby would come, I pretty much had to take it day by day. Sometimes hour by hour.

If I was anxious about not knowing when my baby was going to be born, I asked myself whether I was in labour in that moment.no? then I let go of the worry. I simply observed this worry as part of my process for preparing to meet my little one.

Fears that my baby will suffer.

Another common source of anxiety for me was the possibility that my baby might suffer or experience pain. Even though I considered my baby's potential for suffering when I made the decision to continue, those fears still haunted me. After all, how can my baby have a life-limiting condition and not suffer? Don't fatal diseases and deformities hurt? Could labour or birth be traumatic? Is death painful? And what if my baby survives for a while- ill his quality of life be so poor that my decision to continue inadvertently causes undue suffering? all these questions went through my head when I had to make the decision to continue, I was told baby's like kaiden do not feel pain and are more than likely deaf, blind, and unconscious.

I worried that my baby was in pain, I worried that he would suffer during the birth.

I was afraid my baby would be born alive and then struggle for life in my arms. I was afraid that this baby who was so very sick would not find a peaceful death.

I worried that he would be in pain, especially toward the end as his body "realised" that something was not right and would begin to shut down. My medical caretakers assured me that he would not be in pain.

The overriding worry was whether or not, if he were born alive, he would have pain. The only reason I ever questioned carrying him to term was that I was petrified he would be in pain, and I could not bear that. I really felt like as his mother, it was my responsibility to protect him from pain, and I worried that my decision was not doing that.

Fears about my baby's appearance

I also worried about what my baby would look like. Would I reach out to hold my little one or would I recoil in fear? Especially because my baby's condition was outwardly visible, I was frightened.

I was truly afraid of what kaiden would look like. anencephaly is not very pretty to look at, and I was afraid of my reaction once id seen him.

My doctor tried to reassure me, but I now know that it was normal to worry about my baby's appearance and how it would affect me. To cope, I separated my imagination from reality. Instead of dwelling on what I was imagining – which was much worse than the actual reality- I went ahead and researched the facts. By learning more during my pregnancy, my baby's appearance was less shocking and destressing to me after birth.

I was terrified that I would have haunting memories of my baby if I looked at him.

After looking at pictures of baby's with kaidens condition in medical books, I felt comforted. they are still beautiful babies.

After looking at pictures of other babies with anencephaly, I worried about how my baby would look. I knew that I would love him with all my heart no matter what, but how was my baby going to look? After looking at many pictures over time, they got easier, and I knew that he would be beautiful.

Worries about my baby's appearance was a natural consequence of being given information that focused solely on my baby's abnormalities, ignoring my baby's normal features. I asked the technician to point out familiar and normal body parts to me. I also remembered that when I meet my baby, I would be looking through the eyes of love, and like most parents, I seen something in my child that was beautiful, he was perfection to me.

Fears about death

I was fearful of meeting death. What will it be like to hold my dying baby? Will my decisions about medical intervention still feel right? Will he have died peacefully? These fears I had were natural and common.

I was concerned about watching my baby die since I had never witnessed a death before. I also was not sure if I would be able to help myself from feeling like I wanted to do more to save him.

When I was afraid of the dying process, I asked my doctor to describe the details and what to expect. I joined Facebook support groups and I talked to other anencephaly moms about their experience. Hearing it from other parents cleared up my misconceptions and it reassured me that it can be peaceful and loving experiences.

While fears were a natural part of my journey, I need not be ruled out by them. I accepted that my worries for my baby's comfort were just a natural expression for my parental devotion. Even in the face of reassurances, I still remained worried – and that is okay too.

Techniques for coping

I found myself unable to move past despair even fleetingly, I felt stuck in a rut of grief, I felt overwhelmed by the wild swings, I simply wished that I would feel better so that I could open myself up to my baby's presence, there was a number of techniques I tried.

A particularly effective way of dealing with my stressful situation was to practice cognitive techniques, such as reframing and mindful acceptance, that are based on the idea that how I think about a situation affects how I feel about it.

I noticed that when all I thought about was how terrible the pregnancy was, all I felt was terrible. But whenever I thought about how continuing my pregnancy also gave me the opportunity to nurture my baby, I felt some joyful anticipation. Likewise, I chastised myself for feeling terrible and got myself down for feeling okay when my baby was not- I was only adding to my distress. Whenever I accepted the ebb and flow of all my feelings, I could move on with my experience instead of struggling against it. by focusing on the positives and going with the flow were two ways of reducing my distress.

Reframing involves countering distressing thoughts with positive ones. To give this a try, I purposely countered a distressing thought with a positive one. for instance, I was dwelling on what a tragic hand I was dealt, I than tried considering how much love and appreciation I had for that child, or I imagined nurturing, life infirming activities such as bathing and dressing my little one after birth. But if I felt overrun by distressing thoughts and incapacitated by misery, I deserved some respite. I was not trying to banish my painful thoughts: I was just trying to find a balance that was less agonizing for me. whenever I could focus on the positive aspects of this gift of time, I found some relief.

Mindful acceptance involved paying attention to what was going on inside me and around me, in the moment, nonjudgmentally. I observed my thoughts and feelings, however positive or negative, and I accepted them as a natural part of my experience with my child. I practiced mindful acceptance and it enabled me to let my feelings flow through me without fighting or avoiding them. This gave me compassion for myself and my family and a sense of peace about my journey.

Both techniques helped me be more psychologically flexible and therefore resilient in the face of stress. By becoming proficient in these cognitive techniques required practice, particularly because I was changing deeply ingrained habits, but I see results quickly.

The power of reframing and mindful acceptance was that even though I knew my situation and my grief would not change, I could change the way I behold the landscape and to feel less overwhelmed and better balanced.

Spiritual and philosophical aspects

As I tried to comprehend my baby's fate, I had a whirlwind of questions, not just about my baby's condition but larger questions: spiritual questions about God, fate, the universe, the meaning of life. Pondering and questioning my beliefs was a normal part of coming to terms with my situation. asking "why?" was poignant and frustrating. I felt angry that my prayers were not being answered.

I remember screaming in the bathroom one night. When my mam came in to see what was going on, I screamed, and she held me. I was so angry and terrified. I kept asking God if this is what I deserved for being such a terrible person. I figured that god was punishing me and I hated him for it.

I was wondering in the back of my mind: why? I struggled with that a lot, yet at the same time I knew God was in control of it all.

I searched for spiritual and philosophical comfort. I found solace in the thought that there were ways of being that have a purpose that I cannot yet understand. I had faith that that path was my destiny. I came to accept that whatever happened was ultimately in the best interests of me and my baby. I reclaimed some of my personal power and I decided that I would get through this.

I coped by praying and hanging onto my faith like a life raft. I also realized I had to figure this out for myself and that nobody could do this for me.

I think that when I finally surrendered and began to pray for God to do what is best for my baby, things were tolerable. It was when I asked God to have this baby be born now, or to give him a miracle, that I just could not cope. I had to admit that it was out of my control and plead that god take care of my child, because I just could not.

Several people have told me that I am the perfect parent for kaiden. That is the best compliment I have ever been given. it is a great honour and privilege to be his mother. I love him so much my heart often aches. He has thought me to live and love more deeply. I am more deliberate in the choices I make. I want to live a purposeful life and be reunited with him in heaven. Knowing that I   was going to lose him forced me to focus on what is truly important in life. I hate to think of how much of my life I have wasted on unimportant and insignificant troubles.

I felt that others did not really "get it". I felt that ultimately their prayers had nothing to do with kaiden or me; it was between the person praying and God. and so, I was alone in my understanding. But not lonely! I felt strong, empowered, and eventually, as I practiced being present with my baby, and, as I realized how tentative incipient life can be, I felt increasingly grateful that I had him growing in my belly at all.

For so many weeks, I struggled because I had been looking at my baby through the lens of the diagnosis and not as a creation of God. It was during an ultrasound that I fully realized that no matter the diagnosis, no matter the cause, kaidens malformations were no accident, no mistake, my child was beautiful and loved since even before his beginning.

Living in the twilight of death

I prayed for a miracle and at the same time I planned his funeral.

One of the most challenging aspects of continuing my pregnancy was the fact that I was essentially living in the shadow of death, sometimes I felt like the coffin, carrying my baby that was doomed. How could I make plans when I did not know which day was going to be my baby's last? how could I enjoy the time I had with my baby when I was consumed with grief? how could I proceed, when moving through time only brought me closer to my baby's final hour?

Over time, my grief softened, and it allowed me to embrace that foreknowledge. then I shifted my focus toward using that awareness to me and my baby's advantage. Even though knowing ahead was going to be painful, it was a blessing because it informed how I used the time remaining. I used it wisely and lovingly.

As I adjusted to living in the twilight, I attained a sense of acceptance too. I did not like it or succumb to it, but I just went with the flow of it. When my baby's survival was out of the question, there was no struggle for finding the magic cure. Instead, there was a sense of surrender to something bigger than me. Death lurking in the shadows felt horrific at first. As I adjusted to my baby's reality, my shock and horror began to fade, I began to focus on how precious each day was. preparing for death also meant appreciating my baby's life to the fullest.

Reclaiming hope

While others viewed my situation as hopeless, my hopes did not disappear – they evolved from hoping my baby would survive to hoping that my baby would die peacefully, surrounded by love. I hoped that my baby would feel loved, that my baby would be acknowledged, that my baby would be remembered. these were profound kinds of hope.

At first, I clinged on to my hopes for the best outcome possible or envision what could be right or go well, it was natural to hope for a miracle, a diagnostic error, or a baby who beats the odds.

I wanted God to perform a miracle for kaiden. I wanted the doctors to be wrong.

There was always that bit of hope that I held on to that maybe the next ultrasound showed a prognosis that was not as serious as they thought. there was denial and a secret hope that it might have been the first-ever incorrect anencephaly diagnosis, maybe his head was just small? I used to think to myself. Well, how dumb was I.

I hoped that he would be born crying and peeing; I was so ready to fall to the ground and praise god for healing my son. I hoped for him to be a true miracle baby. I hoped for myself that I, as well as my family, would be able to move forward from this.

Even as I held onto hopes for a miracle, my hopes shifted toward making the best of what was more likely to unfold. My dreams were as simple – and powerful- as I hoped for a live birth, a few minutes to whisper some loving words, a comfortable life.

I hoped my baby would beat the odds, it was a fantasy, and in reality, all I wanted was for my baby to be born alive even if it were only for a short time so that I could see him before he died. I wanted to celebrate his life no matter how short it was.

I wanted to see him breath, I wanted to hold him, I just wanted to be able to tell him I loved him.

After reading a story about a baby with minor anencephaly lived for a year, I thought, a year would be nice. I imagined as long as possible with my baby would be a nice, even a day would be nice, any time that was longer than the time I was given would have been nice.

I remember one time I prayed to God, I asked him for ten seconds, just to have him born alive. I did not want to be greedy. I just asked to see him open his eyes, I wanted to see his eyes. I said "I don't care if this is selfish. I do not care if this is not in your plan. I want ten seconds. let me see his eyes.".

Hopes helped allay my fears. whatever I was afraid of, I held onto the hope that my experience would unfold in the best ways possible. I figured out what was important to me, and I fervently wished for that particular outcome.

I hoped that he would not feel pain. I hoped that I would be able to look at him and not be disgusted or afraid of him. I hoped he would look beautiful to me. I hoped he would cry, that I could hold him alive. I hoped it would bring my family closer together.

My dreams were that he would at least be born alive and that I would not go to a prenatal check-up and have no heartbeat. It seemed to me that having him born alive would validate the experience that I went through, the fact that I bothered to carry him. It felt like in other people's eyes it would make

him more real. I could say he lived, he has a name, he deserved a funeral.
I soon stopped hoping for the impossible, even though it was natural, I started thinking about reality.
My last hope in the end for kaiden was that he would have an eternal life in heaven.

2nd amnio-drainage

On the 15^{th of} October 2018, exactly a week after I was sent home in hospital still in pain. I was taken into hospital my ambulance, I had extreme pains, even worse than the last two times, I was having contractions.

I was twenty-six weeks pregnant; I was so big I could barely lift myself off of my bed. I was crying, hyperventilating, I could not breath, I had extreme pain throughout my whole body. I was rushed straight into the emergency room in a wheelchair, they checked my baby's heartbeat, and it was still beating. my specialist rushed down to the emergency room and brought me straight up where he performed an emergency amnio drainage, my amniotic fluid had grown too much. I looked like I was about to burst according to the specialist. The specialist drained nearly four litres of fluid from my womb nearly twice the amount from my first one. the specialist explained that he did not know the fluid in my womb would increase so much and so fast, if he had known that he would have done the amnio drainage the week earlier where I stayed in hospital for the pain of it, he explained that every time he does an amnio drainage the quicker the fluid would increase so he wanted to wait until I could not bear it anymore. I was given two tylex like the last time, I also had to stay overnight with my mam.

After my first amnio drainage I felt such relief, I was out of pain, but I was still uncomfortable, sill in pain. how could I complain, my baby was still alive? I felt as though I was being selfish for feeling in pain, I could only imagine how my baby felt.

I could not sleep, I was tossing and turning, I decided to get up for a shower with the aid of my mama, I nearly collapsed with the surge of pain that I got as soon as I stepped on my feet. My mam called the nurses and they laid me down on the bed, they observed that my body had gotten immune to tylex and that it was not working as effectively as it had and they ran out of the room and grabbed a tray with a biohazard bucket and an injection, a pethidine injection. Pethidine is an opioid, it is a similar drug to morphine, its injected into the muscle of your leg or buttock, its effective for only three hours.

The nurse injected the pethidine into my leg and a anti nauseous injection into my other leg, and I instantly felt relief, the pain had disappeared fully within twenty minutes of receiving it, I was able to sleep, finally. I was still given tylex every 6 hours. I woke up the next day with still no relief just like the several days after, I stayed in hospital for a week, receiving pethidine and tylex everyday just to keep my pain at bay.

Amniocentesis result

The amniocentesis results were sent back to the maternity hospital from the lab in England. The results were that there were no chromosomal abnormalities, I got the closure that I needed, my baby was indeed very special and rare.

The amniocentesis also confirmed that my baby was a boy, it confirmed that I had a son. I remember me and my mam reading the results and looking at each other laughing "he's definitely a boy" we said to each other smiling and laughing.

In that moment we did not care about the amniocentesis results nor his chromosomes, in that moment it was about love, the love we all had and still have for kaiden. We were just overjoyed that I was having a son, for definite.

Spending the rest of my pregnancy in hospital

Once I got my second amnio drainage my overnight stays in the hospital were never ending, I got my junior cert results whilst in hospital.

My dad was allowed to collect my results from my school early, he rang me laughing teasing me saying "are you ready, are you ready", the midwives and nurses I got to know whilst staying in there, all gathered around my room, they got me a card wishing me luck signed from all of them, the social worker brought me chocolate and jellies and a card, the bereavement counsellor got me a card and gathered around my room also. It was a special moment.

From spending so much time in hospital, I figured out what I wanted to be in the future, a midwife.

I got my results, and everybody was overjoyed for me, I passed every subject no matter how much was going through my head, no matter how sick or nausea I was, I passed everything. I got to go to Joel's restraint with my family that night. The midwives kept on telling me that will be working alongside them in a few years, it became my biggest goal, and I am currently doing my leaving cert course, three years after I had kaiden to accomplish my dream and to make him proud. Nearly every week I was in and out of hospital for days on end. I started to become depressed.

Did I want to go into labour early?

All I could think of whilst in hospital was how much I wanted to get out of it, I was sick and tired of the sickness, the pain, the hospital bed, the constant medications just to keep me comfortable.

I confronted my specialist and asked him was it possible for me to be induced, I told him that I just wanted it all to be over. He sat me down and told me that its technically terminating a pregnancy and in 2018 "abortion" was still illegal. I just wanted to have my baby.

My specialist told me that there could be exceptions, if the mother's life or health is in danger, he took in the way that I was, the pain that I was in.

He called a meeting that evening with all the head foetal medicine doctors and midwifes to consider my question, but it was denied.

All they could do for me is to keep me comfortable.

The anaesthesiologist

The day after I was denied ability to have my child early, the anaesthesiologist paid me a visit.

Physician anaesthesiologists specialize in anaesthesia care, pain management and critical care medicine.

He explained to me that he was worried for me, talking about addiction, he explained that for every day I was in the hospital, I was given at least one dose of pethidine. He explained that pethidine is highly addictive, it is an opioid, he became concerned for me.

He told me that the nurses noticed that my body was starting to become immune to pethidine, that was why I was receiving it nearly twice a day.

He took pethidine off my prescription and swapped it for 10mg of oxynorm a morphine tablet.

My momma shower

On the 29th of September 2018, I was having a miserable day, it was a gloomy, rainy day. I could barely get up out of the bed.

My dad asked me did I want to go on a drive to Blessington lakes and get ice cream. I agreed straight away to go, it is one of my childhood memories, always going down to the lake. it was always a place of escape, I felt free throwing and skipping stones into the lake.

We went and got ice cream, but even though I did not get out of the car because of the weather I still felt free, I felt peace, my head was clear of all troubles and worries.

We arrived home and I got out of the car just wanting to lie in bed, depressed, my thoughts and minds were taking control of me. I opened the kitchen door to a crowd of my family friends shouting "surprise", my mam and family had set up a "momma shower", for me. I was ecstatic with joy. I could not believe it no matter how much I had dreamed of a gender reveal or baby shower, but I felt it would not be right or just, this party was in celebration of

me, we played games, I got lots of care packages and gifts from family and friends.
One of the most special things I received was a large hardback copy with lots of notes and letters to me from everyone who was at the party.
It felt like a normal pregnancy for once.
I enjoyed the life that was in me, I felt appreciated, my baby was appreciated.
I am so grateful to have such a supportive family and a group of supportive friends by my side.

Palliative care for my baby

I met with the palliative care team when I was around 30 weeks pregnant.

I understood that it was getting really close to my baby's arrival, it was getting very close to saying hello and goodbye in nearly the same breath.

No matter how hard it was I knew I needed to make plans for my baby's care.

Palliative care is care designed to make a life-limiting condition as comfortable and symptom free as possible when it is clear that further treatment aimed at cure is neither possible nor effective.

I knew my baby would not be in pain, it was just about his comfort.

They talked to me about skin to skin straight after birth, which calms the heartbeat.

They talked to me about my baby not being able to eat but if he does live long enough, I can give him sucrose solution on his lips, and he will lick it off with the sugary taste.

I had to choose a godparent for kaiden, if I wished my baby to be christened straight after birth, which I did.
It was hard, probably one of the hardest meeting of my pregnancy, but I knew that it was essential.

My last bereavement counsellor meeting

I was 31 weeks pregnant when I had my last bereavement counsellor meeting, the 19th of October 2018.

It was a depressing meeting, not one bit of laughter nor happiness.

It was planning my babies' birth, death, burial, and funeral plans.

I picked out my baby's "angel gown", which he would be buried in, I picked out a white gown which had a blue waistcoat attached onto it, it was perfect for my baby and I knew once I seen it that it was the only right one for my baby, we were given 6 angel gowns a small, medium, and large size in a blue and silver colour, nobody knew how big or small he would be.

I wanted to have a normal funeral mass for him. I knew that that is what I wanted.

I wanted to have a vaginal birth with only gas and air, no epidural. I wanted to experience every little detail of my labour and birth.

I wanted to bring him home for a day and the next day would be the day I bury him.

We organised the fealican memory boxes, the footprint and handprint imprints and the professional photographs from another charity called now I lay me down to sleep (NILMDTS), all free of charge, I was amazed at this, I was happy and sad at the same time. Me and my mam also booked hand and footprint castings off a girl we found on Facebook which come in a lovely picture frame where I could place a picture of him also in with the castings of his hands and feet with a plaque with his name on it.

My bereavement counsellor also told me that the hospital provides a white coffin for my baby with a silver plaque with my baby's name and death of birth/death.

We picked a godfather for kaiden, my little brother Darragh.

Getting closer to birth

The remaining weeks of the pregnancy went fast, too fast, and I found myself feeling panicky when I would think of the impending birth. I could not slow down the clock, even though I tried. I kept doing things with kaiden that I had always done such as tapping my stomach and him kicking back and singing to him, sometimes I felt like I could not do them enough. All the while knowing that what I did in the remaining weeks would have to last me a lifetime.

As birth and death got closer, I just tried to get through the days without thinking too much. Reminders came more and more frequently, though. Kaiden was quite the kicker, and I could sometimes even see kicks coming through my tummy.

I tried to be "normal", doing my hair and makeup every day, getting dressed, putting on a happy face, and inquiring into the wellbeing of others, but my heart was broken in a million little pieces, and I had no idea how I was going to say goodbye to a baby whom I loved so much. I had no idea how I was going to live the rest of my life without this little boy in it.

In the final weeks of my pregnancy, with my overriding wishes carefully considered, medical decisions made, a birth plan discussed with my caregivers, my family and friends lined up to support me, I felt logistically prepared. I felt partially intellectually prepared, medically prepared, even spiritually prepared. But was it normal to feel unprepared emotionally? All I could do was experience my baby's birth and short life in the moment. That was also the beauty of it.

I felt a sense of resolution and peace about decisions and plans that I made. I felt like I had all my bases covered and confident that whatever scenario played out, I would be able to manage it.

During the last few weeks before kaiden was born I really felt at peace about my decision for comfort care. If I was blessed to have some time with him alive, I just wanted to enjoy every minute with him – to hold him and cuddle him and stroke his hair.

As the days passed and brought me closer to the day my baby would be born, it seemed that my senses and emotions were heightened. My remaining fears seemed magnified in anticipation.

I could visualize the moments leading up to his birth, but for the actual birth and the moments with him in my arms, I could not go to that place. It was almost as if my mind and heart were protecting me from the most heart-wrenching time in my life. Maybe I would have run away to a beach and tried to stay pregnant forever. I knew the time would be sacred and beautiful. I just could not picture myself going through it.

I knew that as long kaiden was inside of me he was fine. So, the closer I came to delivering, the more afraid I was for him. I did not want him to die or suffer. I wanted him to have a peaceful life, even though it was only going to be very short. I wanted him to feel my love and know that I loved him so very much. I knew that after I delivered, that I would no longer have control of his life.

Though I had prepared myself all pregnancy long for the fact that I would lose him, no amount of preparation could prepare me for a still and lifeless baby. The loss that I soon faced was so overwhelming to me and I had no idea to bear it.

I missed him so much already and he was not even gone yet.

As my due date neared, I wanted to take action to help calm myself or provide some distraction. My friends and family wanted to pitch in for me. Although this time of anticipation was intense, it was also rich. Whether I felt confident or apprehensive, completely ready or wishing that I had a bit more time, I had done what I was able to do to prepare for the big day. That was all that was asked of me.

It was time to meet my baby.

Going into labour

On the night of October 29th, 2018, I was in tremendous pain, I was twisting and turning all throughout the night, the pain that I felt in my hips felt unbearable. I was 33 weeks pregnant at this stage. I had an appointment with the specialist at 2.00pm on the 30th of October 2018, but it was the early hours of the morning, I tried to just bear the pain and wait it out until my appointment. They were not contracting pains, more like really bad pressure in my pelvic area, and my hips were throbbing with shooting pains. It was 6.00am when my partner was getting up for work, I was still awake twisting and turning, I started to cry at the stage where it got intolerable. I decided that I would wake my mam and dad up, they told me to just try and have a sleep, but I could not, I could not even get comfortable. I had not had an amnio drainage in some time, "maybe that's all it is, maybe I just need an amnio drainage" I thought to myself. Maybe it was the fluid making me in so much pain and feeling lots of pressure. I eventually fell asleep; I do not remember how but when I woke up at around 12.30pm the pain had only worsened. I got up, ready and dressed and me, my mam and dad went to the hospital for my appointment. I had asked my dad a few days before hand did, he want to come in to see kaidens ultrasound, it was always just me and my man who attended them because my dad would stay at home watching my little brothers, I also wanted him to come in and see kaidens ultrasound because in reality I did not know when was going to be our last.

This appointment was in the specialist's private clinic which was still on the hospital grounds. The appointment was free of charge. He wanted to do a 4D ultrasound on kaiden. I wondered if I had enough amniotic fluid to do the amnio drainage procedure, I hoped that I did. I was too uncomfortable and too much in pain, it was non-stop chronic pain.

We arrived at the private clinic and we sat and waited , my dad got a work call and left the waiting room but as soon as my dad left , I was called in for my ultrasound , I could not see him anywhere , so me and my mam had no choice but to go in to the scanning room without him , I thought to myself "he could just come to the next one" , but was there a next one… , it hurt me that my dad missed the ultrasound by accident , his last ultrasound but it was not long after being in that scan room that kaiden was in his grandads arms. I see my baby's facial features, his button nose, his eyes, his lips, toes, and fingers. for once I could see, adore, and take in his normal features instead of everyone just focusing on his malformations and deformities. He was still a baby, he still looked like a baby. that was the first time where I had seen his perfect chubby face.

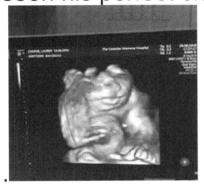

I asked the specialist if he could measure my baby's weight. He said "unfortunately, I cannot.
do that. Usually, we have to measure the head and spine and we cannot do that with kaiden". I was a bit upset, it felt like a slap in the face even though it was not necessary to know his weight. he told me that the midwives

would measure his weight and length as soon as he was born.

I told him about the pain that I was enduring in my hips, sides, and pelvic area. He told me that it was all just pressure from the fluid. he measured the amount of amniotic fluid in my womb, and it was indeed well over normal capacity, he wanted to keep me in overnight to keep an eye on my pain, so he booked me in for an amnio drainage procedure, my 3rd one for 7.00pm that evening. We already had all of our hospital bags in the car as we thought I would be kept in. the specialist checked me in, and we were brought straight into my normal room on the fourth floor of the hospital. I was given a dose of oxynorm, and I fell asleep, I had a good sleep knowing that my pain was going to be all over soon.

I was awoken and told that the specialist was free to do the amnio drainage procedure, an hour before scheduled, 6.00pm. we went, and the specialist did the amnio drainage. I was certain that I was mentally and physically prepared to have my baby, I wanted to have him, I remember whilst being pushed in the wheelchair down to the procedure, I whispered to my mam "third time lucky", to go into labour as that was one of the risks of getting to procedure done. He did the procedure and drained 3 litres of fluid from my womb, I was still feeling pressure and pain, but   the specialist prescribed me a sleeping tablet to help me have a good night sleep, especially after my procedure, I had a small bit of dinner and went straight asleep, the tablet I was given made me feel very sleepy. Usually, my mam tells me that after any of my amnio drainage procedures I usually go straight asleep and that I usually do not wake up, not even to go to the toilet but the next morning my mam told me that I was still twisting, turning, and groaning in pain, even after the amnio drainage where the specialist drained 3 litres of fluid, even after the sleeping tablet, me and my mam found that very unusual.

When the doctor was doing her rounds, my mam called her in to my room, I explained to the doctor how much pain I was in, it was a different sort of pain that I was feeling, none like the rest.

The doctor put on a glove to examine my cervix, I was 2cm dilated, I was not in active labour. The doctor explained how I was not in active labour and that I could have been 2cm for the past couple of days or weeks even, the doctor could not say I was in labour or that I got 2cm dilated from the amnio drainage because my cervix was not examined when I first came into the hospital the day before. She wrote a prescription to give me a dose of pethidine. I received the pethidine, and I did not feel one bit better. What I needed was a steamy hot shower, which I had. I laid in bed and the pain only grew stronger, I started to cry, and my mam started to laugh with her nerves, I shouted at her "don't you laugh at me" whilst she still continued to laugh. I got up whilst my mam held my arm, I walked up and down the corridor. I needed to sit down again. I told the nurses to call the doctor to examine me, the doctor said that she was not checking me as she knew I was not in labour. all the hospital staff were convinced that it was just the Braxton hicks I was experience, but I knew it was different. I got in for another shower, I could not walk with my legs closed. I sat down on the bed, and I felt as though I was sitting on a watermelon, I screamed as loud as I could, my poor mam did not know what to do. My mam walked me to the bathroom and as I looked down, my mucus plug came out on my underwear, I remember saying to my mam "is that it, is that it", the nurse confirmed it was my mucus plug but the doctor still did not want to examine me. I was than given a second dose of pethidine, I could not lie down, I could not sit up, I could barely walk. Every surge of pain was getting more intense and closer together. me and my mam walked up and down the corridor as best as I could. The midwifes put me on a drip of paracetamol for my pain, yeah … paracetamol. I could not take the pain anymore and I demanded the doctor, any doctor to come up and examine me. the doctor agreed and as she examined my cervix she shouts "oh … your six ½ cm dilated", I knew that my baby was coming all along, when nobody else did. They got me a wheelchair as fast as they could and rushed me down to the delivery room. From 11.00am to 2.00pm I had gone from 2cm dilated to six ½ cm dilated. I facetimed my partner as I was being pushed in the wheelchair, he started laughing thinking it was a joke, whilst my mam rang my whole family.

Whilst being pushed in the wheelchair down to the delivery ward, reality hit me. Only then did I feel unprepared, so unprepared. My thoughts were racing. "What happening, lord? why are you allowing this to happen now?", I could not believe that it was happening, my baby was going to be here soon, my baby was going to die. I was petrified, yet I was joyful to meet the life, the little boy that had been growing inside of me, he was already a fighter. "What would he look like? Is he going to be alive? I hope he is alive; I want to see his eyes and hear him cry." So many thoughts racing through my mind. Whilst going through the doors entering the delivery ward, I whispered to myself "here we go".

Giving birth

we got into the delivery room, the butterfly room was the room I was in. the midwives rushed and asked me did I want an epidural, I denied it, I just wanted the gas and air. the midwife examined me whilst I had a contraction and she shouted, "she is fully dilated". I was screaming crying, I started shouting "I want the epidural" but the midwife told me it was too late, the pain was becoming unbearable, I did not how I was going to get through it.

My waters had not broken yet, so the midwife needed to break them for me, I was not ready to have my waters broken, my dad came into the room and said that everybody was outside, everybody was outside to meet my baby, I knew than that my baby truly did matter, my baby was loved.

I kept on telling the midwife I needed to go to the toilet, she knew then that I was ready to push, I agreed for them to break my waters in that moment. On each side of me was my mam and my bereavement counsellor and in front of me was two midwives and a doctor. After two pushes my baby's head was out, my bereavement counsellor took my hand and brought it in between my legs where my baby's head was, I felt instantly connected to my baby, it felt weird at first, it did not feel real, but it was one of the purest moments I had ever felt in my life. After six more long, hard pushes he was here.

Kaiden~rhys Paul cooper
Born 2.59pm
31st October 2018
2lbs 12oz

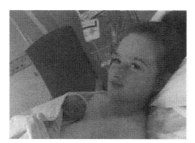

As soon as he was out, the midwives put a blanket around my baby and wrapped gauze around the opening of on his head and then checked his heartbeat, he was alive, my baby was alive, even though his heartbeat was weak, it was still there.
The bereavement counsellor said to me "will we just double check to see if he is definitely a boy", we all let out a giggle.

In that moment I felt no sadness, I felt no worry, it was almost magical, nothing but pure and utter love.

As the midwife handed him to me, all I could see was how perfect he was. I looked at my mam and I said "mam, that's my baby, that's my boy ", she replied "he sure is" whilst she stroked my hair while admiring his beauty. All anyone had been telling me throughout my whole pregnancy was all about everything that was wrong with him, his malformations, his deformities. no one had told me that I would look at him and fall instantly and totally in love with him.

I remember being so gentle with him and his head. I was told to speak to him whilst they delivered my placenta. I held his hands and admired his wrinkly toes. my baby was still and silent, but he was still there.

I whispered to my baby "I love you; can you hear me; do you recognize my voice." I did not really know what to say. I could see my baby was tired, he had fought for so long, I remember saying to him with tears rolling down my face" it's okay son, I'm here, you can let go, it's okay to let go", they were not sad tears , I could not save him from his faith and I came to terms with it in that moment whilst looking at his innocent self when before it felt impossible to come to terms with anything . all I could do was to be there for him, to make sure he felt safe and loved.

I got myself covered up and my family came in, not just my dad and brothers but my aunties and uncles and cousins, with two bottles of prosecco. I cried with happiness, everybody got to hold and admire kaiden before the hospitals Chaplin came in and christened kaiden. It was just like a normal christening with celebrations of a cup of prosecco afterwards, my baby really did matter.

I remember looking at everyone hold kaiden and them all being consumed with love. I just loved him so much. Even with anencephaly and his omphalocele, he was perfect. So beautiful. I truly cannot put into words how much love I felt for him.

I was bursting with new-parent emotions: joy, pride, amazement, wonder exhaustion – and most of all, consuming, intoxicating love.

I still felt his tiny heartbeat on my chest, I remember looking down at him and he had moved his hand and he had started to suck his thumb, my baby was sucking his thumb. It was such a joyous but heart-breaking moment also.

We captured everything, every small detail. His hands, feet, me and kaiden, his christening, family members holding him. We made sure not to miss a single moment, they would be all I had left.

A different foetal medicine doctor to my normal specialist came in the room. She said to me "I am sorry for your loss", my baby was not even dead yet, not that we knew of. She picked him off my chest and I see his right eye open and close, I got to see my baby's eyes. A couple of minutes after the foetal medicine doctor looked at him and checked his heartbeat, she walked around to me and handed me my baby and said, "I'm sorry, he has passed". I knew than that my baby opened his eyes to look at his mam before he went to heaven.

My "warrior"

Kaiden~rhys Paul cooper

31st October 2018
2.59pm ~ 4.45pm
2lbs 12oz

Everybody had left to go up to my room on the fourth floor to give me a few minutes alone with my son.

I remember when I was shopping for kaidens cloths, when I picked out the dinosaur outfit I said to my mam "imagine I had him on Halloween, I'd have to put him in that" and so it only felt right that I stuck to my plan.

My mam ran up and got the dinosaur outfit for me and one of the nurses on the ward helped me dress him as I could not touch his omphalocele or the opening in his head, I was all too gentle with him. even though he was in  heaven, and he could not feel any pain I was still worried that I might hurt him, motherly instincts were already starting to kick in. I carried my baby in his blue blanket with his name on it in my arms while I was pushed in a wheelchair up to my room.

I laid in bed whilst everybody could not get enough of him, I was given gifts such as new pyjamas, slippers, facemasks, and my baby got gifts also, a silver christening bracelet with his name and date of birth on it from my uncle Derek, he also got lots of teddy bears.

My younger brothers left the hospital as I told them to go trick or treating for me and bring me in a goodie bag the next day, my youngest two brothers did not really understand entirely what was going on, they stayed in my uncle Derek's house and went trick or treating with my cousins.

My dad stayed until around 7.30pm with my other brothers Jonathan and Darragh.

I took several photos of kaidens features, pictures of his presents, of his bed, of the room, of me and him, of him and my mama, everything that I could take pictures of I took pictures of.

My baby was still warm, I prepared myself for him to be cold, he still had his plush pink skin and lips and cheeks. My baby's Moses basket which was beside my bed had a special cooler underneath it, to help preserve my baby's body, I guess.

I was given another sleeping tablet that night to help me sleep.

I than got in for a shower and got in to clean pyjamas.

I held, kissed, and snuggled him until my body gave up with the tiredness, I did not want to put him down., but I needed to sleep as the next day would be a big day for memory making, I would be bathing him, getting his castings done, his foot and handprints done, and professional photographs taken.

The next day would be the day were my partner and my friends would meet kaiden alongside with my family coming up as well, again.

My baby would have a small ceremony for him in the hospitals chapel and in the hospitals, chapel was a book, a memorial book of all the baby's names who passed away in the hospital. The babies name is written on the page of their date of birth alongside a small message from their parent/s, I had to think of what message to write. every day the page of the book is turned and each year on the 31st of October my baby's name alongside with the message I wrote is on the opened page of the book.

I fell asleep, longing for the morning to come quicker, just so I could mother my baby as best as I could, I wanted to mother him as much as possible.

It still felt like just a big blur to me, it did not feel real, I kept waking up in the middle of the night and just looking to my left to see my baby, my son. I would kiss him, rub his cheeks, and tucked him in to make sure he was cosy.

Memory making

I woke up the morning after birthing my son, the day for all our memory and keepsake making. I remember sitting myself up slowly, I rubbed my eyes and stretched, I looked to my left, and I see my baby boy, cold and still lying next to me in the little Moses basket. It felt like it was all the dream. I was ecstatic to have my son and to finally have him in my arms. Yes, I knew he was in heaven, I knew he passed away, but he was still beside me, I could still hold and kiss him. His physical body was lying next to me, and I knew that in the next day or two even his physical body would be taken from me, he would be gone forever. I could not face the thoughts of letting him go, I could not think about that. I did not want to let him go, not so quick. I wanted to keep him here with me forever. I knew that once he was taken from me and that coffin lid closed that I would never see him again until it is my time to walk up the stairs of heaven to see him awaiting for me at the gates.

I had a small bit of breakfast, and I got to dress my baby with help of a nurse, I dressed him in the blue teddy bear dungaree set that I had bought him, and white bunny rabbit baby sock boots I had bought in the hospitals shop on the bottom floor.

she also wrapped fresh gauze around my

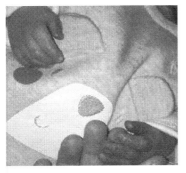

baby's head. It was around 11.00am and a lady in which I found off Facebook that does 3d castings of baby's hands and feet was due in at 2.00pm to do kaidens, a couple of days before I had kaiden I saw her Facebook page and I was embarrassed and upset to ask her could she do my baby's castings, I had to tell her my baby was going to be dead, I was afraid she would decline because I am sure every other one of her appointments were filled with joy and laughter and trying to get a crying, wiggly baby's toes into the mould , that's what she was used to while my baby was going to be silent , cold and still but after her hearing my story she asked me could she do it for me free of charge. Soon after I dressed kaiden I got a message off the lady saying she cannot make it, I was very upset, I thought that she was obviously uncomfortable or too nervous to do my babies castings.

My bereavement counsellor came into my room with a box. The box was from the Irish charity fealican. Inside the box was full of keepsakes, including a teddy bear with a purple ribbon to put in my baby's bed with him, a memorial book to put in his name, date of birth, a picture and invisible ink wipes and paper sheets to get hand and footprints. It came with a small candle, helpful leaflets and books for memory making and grieving, a book for grieving mothers and "angel" body wash for my baby's bath.

Me and my bereavement counsellor helped each other to do kaidens hand and foot prints. Not long after that my partner came up to visit me and kaiden in hospital, he brought a bag of goodies as usual, and my partner met my baby. my partner held kaiden, but I could see he was nervous and quite shocked. My partner left after spending around two hours with me and kaiden as him and my family had not met fully.

I was determined to remember everything about him and make concrete memories, impressions on my mind and soul that I could carry with me for the rest of my life.

One of my most cherished memories is that of me and my bereavement counsellor very tenderly giving kaiden his first and last bath after he died. The bereavement counsellor brought a special baby bath on wheels into my room so I could give my baby a bath, I did not know whether I was going to be allowed or able to give my baby a bath, it was one of the purest experiences I have ever felt. The sun streamed through the window, and I felt the warmth on my face as I bathed my son with the "angel" shampoo that I had gotten in my memorial box. I was still afraid I was going to hurt him or burst the omphalocele which would not happen, but the worry took control over me, and I held back, I let my

bereavement counsellor do the rest. My mam was in the back recording a picturing every memory making moment. I just remember his chubby legs; his legs were humongous. I dressed my baby in the grey lion outfit as that evening was the professional photographs from the I lay me down to sleep charity and later that day was also the ceremony that was being held for my baby. In the memorial box was two pearl bracelets, two matching ones, one for me and one for kaiden so I put our matching bracelets on also which had teddy bear charms on them.

 I was also able to get a couple of locks of my babies' hair, his hair was Icey blonde.

My mam found a girl on Facebook that was free to come up straight away and do kaidens 3d hand and foot castings. One of my baby's hands and one of my baby's feet was placed into a mould and that all it was, it took five minutes to get the moulds done but it would take six weeks for the whole thing to be finished, I picked out grey castings and a white frame. The hospital also did imprints of my babies' hand and footprints into clay which would take a month to be ready which was also in a white frame but painted blue.

My family and my friends came up to visit me and kaiden again, they all came up for the special ceremony for kaiden also. I do not think I was really thinking that my baby was actually gone, I think I was fooling myself, nothing felt real until my baby's prayer ceremony started, none of the sadness or grief hit me until the prayer ceremony started. I remember during the ceremony all I did was look at my baby and cry, I do not remember what was said in the ceremony, I could not hear anything, the outside world was blurred out in

that moment, we each got a special prayer service card, with kaidens name and date of birth. I snapped out of the sadness as I thought I was wasting time, I had the rest of my life to grieve, the short time that I had with my baby was to be about joy, having my baby here, my first baby and for making memories. After the ceremony everybody except for me and my mam waited outside my room for me to get in for a shower and to get dressed as the photographer was due in the hospital in a half.

hour. I got in for a shower and I got dressed in a pair of jeans, which I have not seen on me in a long time and a nice t-shirt, my mam straightened my hair for me as well.

The photographer arrived and I got lots of photographs taken of just me and kaiden, we got photographs of my whole family and my friends with kaiden too. The photos would be posted out to my house on a USB stick but the women sent five of the photographs to my email so I could pick one of them for my baby's funeral.

After a while everybody left again and it was only me and my mam and dad, my dad bought three of us a chipper takeaway and after we ate my dad left so me and my mam could get a bit of rest after a busy memory making day. I was so happy with how the day went; it was a joyous day. After all every one of the memories I made with my baby that day are now all I have left of him.

The bereavement counsellor arrived back at my room before I went to sleep and gave me another sleeping tablet along with pain medication, she handed me a pen and paper to think of what I wanted written on the memorial book in the chapel under my baby's name. on one of my baby's baby grows it said "mammas star and daddy's son and forever our baby you will be ", I thought that was beautiful so that is what I picked.

Final day/night in hospital

I woke up and looked to my left, my baby was there, it felt like it was a dream still. I just could not believe my baby was here. I could not keep him out of my arms, as soon as I put him down, I would feel terrible and lift him back up and kiss him all over his face. I could not get enough kisses and cuddles. I loved him so much, I love him unconditionally.
The hospitals chaplain came into my room and sat me down, she sat me down to talk to me about plans for my baby and his funeral. She asked me did I want to bring him home, I was over the moon, I said yes definitely straight away, I did not even have to think about it, it was one of the things I would hope to be able to do but if I wanted to bring my baby home, I would have to bring him home the next day and the day after that I would have to bury him. I was outraged "no way" I shouted, it's too early, I need more time with him", I stood up and I started crying, I asked for just one more day, but it would not be right. no matter how much I did not want to

think about, I knew my baby was dead and every dead body starts to decompose after a few days, I knew it was not something nice to think about, but it needed to be taken into consideration, I wanted to remember my baby as he was, I did not want to see my babies physical body "decompose". I agreed that the plan was made for bringing my baby home. that day was going to be my last day in hospital and the day after was the day I got to bring my baby home, and then the day after that was going to be his funeral.

My dad rang bohernabreena cemetery and sorted out my baby's burial. my dad went up to my local church and set up my baby's funeral. The plan was finally made that I was going to bring my baby home on my lap in the car before we would leave the hospital my dad would put the coffin that was specially made for kaiden in the boot of the car. My uncle David sorted out a Moses basket for my house and the hospitals chaplain wanted to do the graveside prayers. We had a brief idea of the coming days ahead.

My last day in the hospital was spent, cuddling, napping, and kissing my baby, I dressed him up for plenty of photos as well.

I did not want to think About the days ahead, so I focused and lived in the moment.

My last day in the hospital was the day for me and my immediate family to have alone time with kaiden, we all had our own unique bonding time with him.

I could not wait to bring my baby home; it was something that I never thought I would be able to do with him.

I was extremely tired that day and night, it had been a really rough and tough few days even though the worse was still to come.

Bringing my baby home

One of the best decisions I ever made was the decision I made to bring kaiden home for a day.

It was pure, I did not have doctors and nurses surrounding me and my child. I got to bring him home just as I would of if he had been healthy and alive even if it were only just for a day.

It meant so much to me to have my baby in my house instead of in a hospital, nobody likes hospitals, and I did not want that to be the only place where I got to mother and make memories with my son.

I woke up in the hospital and dressed my baby in the outfit that I bought him which had "mammys star and daddy's son on it ", this was his going home outfit, I never thought my son would have a going home outfit. The doctors did a final check on me to make sure I was fit enough to go home, and I was fine. I got in for a shower and got dressed into a comfy outfit.

The doctors said that I was due another dose of one of my immunisations, so they gave that injection to me before I left, but as the nurse went to get the injection, I got a phone call off an unknown number. It was a nurse from my local doctors asking when was I available to bring my baby for his heel prick, my face dropped and I started to stutter , I did not know what to say, "sorry I can't bring him to that because he is dead", I could hardly say that so I handed my phone to the midwife that was checking my vitals , I did not even say anything to her , the poor woman did not know who was on the phone. The nurse on the phone gave her sincere apologies, she did not know what had happened kaiden because it did not say anything about my baby's death on the cert or file that does be sent. It was a simple misunderstanding, but it broke my heart, I was holding my baby waiting to get my injection while my dad picked up kaidens coffin and put it in the boot of the car so I could bring my baby home whilst I got that call.

I got my injection and my auntie Michelle swaddled kaiden in one of his soft blankets. I got.

to carry my swaddled baby in my arms through
the hospital, down into the carpark and into my car. I was proud to be kaidens mum and in that moment walking through the hospital I was not scared, I was not embarrassed, I did not care who was looking at me and I did not care what they thought about me. that was one of the proudest moments of my life carrying my baby in my arms out of the maternity hospital and bringing him home. The intrinsic value for me was that I did not have to leave my baby in the hospital without me all by himself. I held him all the way home, and I showed him my house, I showed my room that we would of both slept in. no one ever took him away from me, and that has tremendous value to me now.

As much as I wanted to get home with my baby in my arms, I was anxious to leave the hospital, I was torn by leaving the only place kaidens alive moments were spent. I strangely grew attached to my nurses because they took part in those short, yet very special moments in my life.

At first taking my baby home was a shocking and surprising idea at first. It seemed illegal or somehow unclean – neither of which are true. I simply rocked my baby in the room that would have been ours or we sat quietly on the sofa as a family one last time. My family and friends shared that experience with me.

As soon as I got there, I seen that my nanny had made sandwiches and snacks for kaidens visitors that were coming to my house. Some of my families were already in my house when I arrived. Everybody held kaiden again and we all talked about how much he looked like me, we joked about my labour story, I also boasted to everyone that I gave birth with no epidural but if it were not to late it, I would have gotten it straight away. We all bonded with kaiden and talked to him in our own unique way. We were mesmerizing his beautiful little features, his chubby cheeks, his big double chin, and his fat legs.

An hour or two after I arrived home from the hospital, my uncle David came and set up my baby's Moses basket in the sitting room where I decided me, my brother Darragh and my dad would sleep beside kaiden one last time. I filled the Moses basket with his collection of soft teddy bears. I had also received more gifts from my parent's friends and some family and friends. I got a duplicate of an elephant baby comforter that I had bought kaiden. I decided that when it was time for my baby to be put in his casket, I would give my baby one and I would keep one, it helped me feel more connected to my baby and it made.

everything that was coming less scary to face. When I was at home, the room that my baby was in had to be kept cool and ventilated. My bereavement counsellor advised me. I was also well aware that the appearance of my baby's skin may change during that time.

I had made the decision to give my baby a funeral in my local church. Later on, that day in the evening my local parish priests arrived at my home to arrange my baby's funeral which was to take place at 12.30pm the next day. We talked about songs, picking people out to do readings from the gospel, eulogies and the gifts that would be brought up and put on kaidens coffin to symbolize him and his short life. It was a lot to think about, why I should have to plan my own baby's funeral? I did feel like everything was moving too quickly.

Even after my baby died, caring for my baby's body was entirely normal and natural. I parented my baby not in the way that I wanted to, but I parented him in ways that were uniquely tailored for my baby. Even if I never changed a nappy or given a baby a bath before, even if I felt awkward and unsure, who could have been better to take care of my baby than me?

The angel gown I picked out of the four that I was given was the white angel gown that had the blue waistcoat attached to it in the size medium as the size small was too tiny for kaiden. As handsome as my baby was in the angel gown, I did not want the gown near my baby, I did not want to put him in his "funeral" outfit, his forever outfit. I should not have to do that. I did not want my baby to be in it.

I finally decided on all of the things I needed to pick out for my baby's funeral. I picked out my baby's funeral song which was jealous of the angels by Donna Taggart. That song was also my great grandmother's funeral song who only passed away a couple of months before my baby. The song brings out so much raw emotion. It is an emotional but beautiful song, and I knew it was perfect for my baby. My baby's coffin was already chosen as it was given by the hospital, it was unique and beautiful, it was white with a lace design covering it and two silver angels that were screwed in the top on either end of the coffin, I did not want my baby in that either, God it was hard. I could not face seeing the coffin until the last minute, the minute I had to put my baby in it.

My mother and father ordered personalized flowers and wreaths made from Jackie's florist for my son's grave to put on after his burial, they were blue and white with the word's son, grandson, and nephew.

I also decided on the two people that I wanted to do the readings from the gospel, I chose my auntie Michelle and my brother Darragh who is kaidens godfather. I also made the decision that I wanted to write my own eulogy for my baby's funeral, Something short, sweet, and meaningful. I needed to say something about him, especially because most people in the congregation did not have personal memories of my baby. I wanted the eulogy to serve as an introduction to my baby, a summary of the path we travelled together, an expression of gratitude to those who walked with me, and the testament to the meaning of even a brief life. I was nervous of getting up and speaking by myself in a church full of people, but I knew that I had to, I needed to do it for myself, I did not know whether I was going to be able to do it, but I owed it to him. The three gifts that I chose to symbolize kaiden and his short life were four simple but meaningful things, one of his hats that he had worn, the elephant baby comforter that I had two of, his blue blanket that had stars and his name on it and a photograph of him. I picked my two nannies to bring up the bread and wine up to the alter. I also chose a song that I wanted to be played at my sons' graveside which was ill never love again sang by lady gaga in the movie a star is born because during those few days my life became a "before" and "after" and I did not believe that I could or would ever love again. I sat down at my kitchen table with my baby in my arms, I got a piece of paper out and I got a pen and I started to write my eulogy. I thought very hard about what to write, I knew everything that.

I wanted to say in my head, but I could not put it down on paper, I thought about it for a good amount of time, I was patient with myself. Everything that I truly felt and truly wanted to say could not be emphasised through words nor written on a page, but I wrote my eulogy about my son the best way that I could. Everyone started to leave at about 8.00pm and I got in a shower and got in to fresh pyjamas. I felt so much more comfortable with my baby in my house. I got pillows and duvets to put on the floor and the sofa where me, my dad, and my brother Darragh slept. We held him and kissed kaiden goodnight each at our own time and we got into bed. To be honest I did not want to go asleep, I wanted to stay up all night with him just to spend more time with him. I did not want the day to end as I knew I would have to say goodbye early tomorrow morning, I knew that I would never see him again after that coffin lid closed. I remember trying to go asleep that night and I would jump up and just sit and stare at him whilst he laid still in his Moses basket thinking how much I wished that I could keep him here with me forever. I forced myself to go asleep after a while of twisting and turning but a part of me did not want to wake up the next day, I did not want to face reality, I did not want.

to face my child's funeral mass and burial, I did not want to face the coming day at all.

Kaidens funeral

I remember this day all too well, practically the worst day of my life.

I woke up early, at 8.30am, I just got up and stared at kaidens small body which lay still in the Moses basket, it was my last couple of hours with him and then he would be gone forever. I wanted the ground to swallow me up, I became emotionless that day no able to smile or even cry. I did not have a clue how I was going to get through that day. I held my baby and swaddled him in my arms, I felt like I could not even enjoy swaddling him. I felt so much anger.

I went upstairs and I got dressed into a black shirt and a black skirt with black tights and boots. I asked if everybody that was coming to my baby's funeral would wear an item of blue in honour of my baby. How could this be happening? This is the day I bury my own son, child, that is all I kept on thinking to myself that day. I put a blue ribbon in my hair in honour of my baby. Everybody got dressed and ready for kaidens funeral. it felt like a terrible night.

Planning and having my baby's funeral were one of the most traumatic experiences I have ever went through in my life and probably the most traumatic experience I will ever have to go through. I chose to bury my baby. If someone loses a baby after twenty-four weeks gestation, they have to be buried or cremated by law. I buried my baby at bohernabreena cemetery, in Dublin which is only ten minutes away from my home.

The arrangements that I chose to make to mark my baby's death in the ceremony were very personal to me. I had important religious wishes that I wanted to be observed. I was lucky to be able to do everything that I wanted to do, and I was lucky to share to be able to share it with my family and friends.

It was not something I ever expected to be doing but it was so important to me to mark kaidens life and express some of my grief at losing him.

Watching my dad carrying his coffin over to his burial spot was heart breaking but also such a precious demonstration of love.

Planning the funeral also gave me something to focus on during those first terrible empty days after giving birth to him.

I never thought that I would ever have to bury my own child especially one I never got to know, one I barely got to hold.

Walking through the cemetery with my dad who was holding kaidens coffin will be a feeling that will never leave me.

I remember before my baby's funeral, I asked for a minute to myself with him. I held him and I cried, I cried until no more tears came out. It was gut wrenching; my stomach was doing backflips.

The maternity hospitals chaplain came to my house for help with getting kaiden ready for his funeral, my mother went upstairs and brought down my babies' angel gown. I remember just handing kaiden to my mother and walking out of the sitting room, where we were. My mother and the maternity hospitals chaplain laid kaiden down on the sofa on a blue hand knitted blanket and changed him into the angel gown, I could not even be in the room.

My family and friends came to the house to visit and hold kaiden for one last time. They all took pictures alone with kaiden to keep as memories forever and we took family photos also.

The most traumatizing thing I ever did was not laying kaidens coffin into the ground, it was placing him inside the coffin. I got ten more minutes alone with him before it was "time". The maternity hospitals chaplain and my parents came into the sitting room, I felt as though I did not get enough time with my baby, but no time is ever enough. I could not bear to put my baby in the coffin, I wanted to hold and cuddle him for the rest of my life, it was time to let go but I did not want to let go, not ever. I froze whilst standing there just looking at my baby, in that moment time stood still. I remember everyone's voices going in one ear and out the other, I could not listen to anyone, my mind was a blur. Everybody was trying to comfort me and tell me that it is time to put my baby in his coffin, I was so angry, I broke down and started roaring crying though not a single tear came out of my eye. I was all cried out. I could not put my baby in his coffin, I thought that I would have been strong enough, but I was not. I handed my son over to the maternity hospitals chaplain and she placed him in his white coffin, it was the most emotional time not just for me, for my family also. I glanced at him one last time until his casket lid closed over him forever, even though my baby was dead for the three days prior, but he was not gone until that moment, the maternity hospitals chaplain handed me an angel that was to be screwed on to each end of his coffin, me and my mam closed his casket forever. Everybody left my house to make their way up to the church and I got everything ready that I needed to get ready for the church ceremony.

I will never forget that feeling, that feeling of having a part of me taken away forever. It felt as though half of me was being thorn straight from my cradled arms. When his coffin lid closed part of me was locked away inside of it with him. His closed coffin with his lifeless body laying inside of it was placed on my lip as I sat in the back of my mother and father's car. I tried to let go of my baby in that moment, I said to myself that he is at peace now, I thought it would have made it even a small bit easier in the ceremony and burial, but the truth is I did not let go, I still have not been able to let go nor do I think I ever will. We drove to the church where my baby's funeral was set to take place. I did not know who was going to be there and I did not care who was there in that moment, it was like a big daydream- more like a nightmare. We drove onto the grounds of the church to be surrounded by many people, friends, family, even people whom I never spoke a word to in my life. I see parade of people wearing blue headbands, t-shirts …. Etc, just for my baby. I asked prior to the funeral if anybody could wear blue tokens in memory of my son and they did. In that moment I knew that no matter how short or brief my baby's life was, it still mattered, his short life impacted many others, he left an imprint on this world and on my heart. He was a person, he was born, he was my son and most importantly he was loved, he was loved and still is still loved more than words could ever speak. All my family had a part to play in kaidens funeral service. My nannies brought up the holy bread and wine and My brothers did gospel readings and brought the gifts up to alter which was one of his hats, a blue elephant baby comforter and the group picture of me, kaiden and my family. I chose the songs; I will never love again by lady gaga from a star is born and jealous of the angels by Donna Taggart both songs had meaning and explained exactly how I felt at that time.

Eulogy

Many services include words of Remembrance about the person who has died, especially because most people in the congregation may not have personal memories of your baby these words take on added significance. the eulogy can serve as an introduction to your baby's summary of the path you have traveled together .an expression of gratitude to those who walked with you and a testament to the meaning of even a brief life.

I gave Kaidens eulogy. I did not think I would be able to do it, but I owed it to him.

This is the original eulogy I wrote and said

for my sons funeral

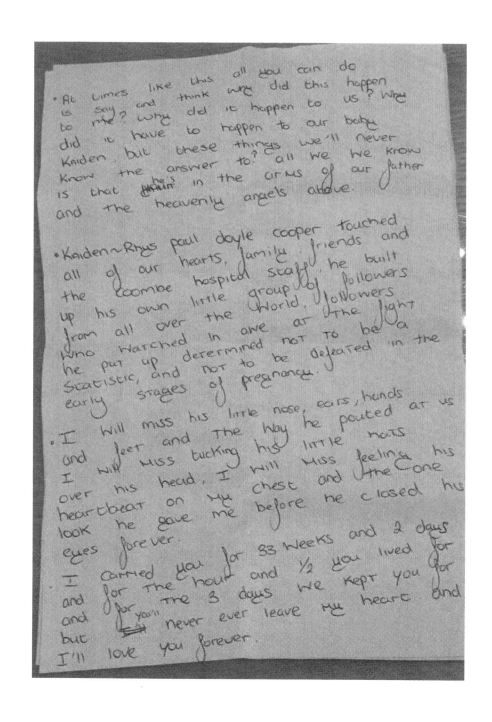

• At times like this all you can do is say, and think why did this happen to me? Why did it happen to us? Why did it have to happen to our baby Kaiden, but these things we'll never know the answer to? all we we know is that he's in the arms of our father and the heavenly angels above.

• Kaiden~Rhys paul doyle cooper touched all of our hearts, family, friends and the Coombe hospital staff, he built up his own little group of followers from all over the World, followers who watched in awe at the light he put up determined not to be a statistic, and not to be defeated in the early stages of pregnancy.

• I will miss his little nose, ears, hands and feet and the way he pouted at us I will miss tucking his little hats over his head, I will miss feeling his heartbeat on my chest and the one look he gave me before he closed his eyes forever.

• I carried you for 33 weeks and 2 days and for the hour and ½ you lived for and for the 3 days we kept you for but you'll never ever leave my heart and I'll love you forever.

After the funeral service.

After the songs were played my two nannies walked up to Kaiden's casket and took off the items which were placed on top of it and the priest blessed kaidens casket with holy water and then my dad lifted his casket and walked out of the church. I was emotionless I did not have any tears left to cry. we got into the car and headed back home.

When we got home we placed his casket in the sitting room, I remember asking my mam could I just open his casket just to even look at him one last time, but I never did, I should just leave him at peace, but I missed him. I sat there with the casket until 12:00pm as his burial was 12:30pm.

Burial service

Burial or scattering the ashes (or if you decide to keep them) is the last step in caring for your baby's body, it is the final physical goodbye. It provided me with a sense of completion and a sense of having carried my baby full circle from life through death watching tenderly every step of way. The gravesite provided lasting physical proof of my baby existence.

Once we were at kaidens plot, we all circled around it and had our chances to express our thoughts through short messages and songs. It is a nice memory for me, even though I was terribly sad. Because it was November, the weather was quite cold, the clouds were out that day and I distinctly remember a moment during kaidens service when the sun peaked out from the clouds and warmed up my cheek. To me it felt like a sign that my son was saying goodbye and that he was going to be okay. When kaidens casket was being put into his grave, I remember standing back behind everyone else and looking away, taking glances little by little until I could not see anything but the freshly dug grave.

Kaiden was my child, even if he only lived eight months in my womb and two short hours in my arms. His life had the same value for me as the life of any other child. Giving him a full funeral and burial was not only what he deserved as a human being, it was a ritual that gave me, as his mother, the closure I needed. His grave is one square meter of official recognition of his existence. I did have a child, he really existed, he is buried here like any other human being who has lived and died.

Everyone who was at the grave side was tearful. It was an all-too-surreal moment. all I wanted was for everyone to leave and I just wanted to lay down there with him and hold him and cry for him to come home to me.

The guilt was so overwhelming when I left his grave I felt like the worst mother in the world for leaving him there and I just thought it was best for me to not look back whilst we drove out of the graveyard.

We had a little get together with family and friends to celebrate kaidens life, no matter how short his life was there were so many people who loved and cared for him.

after kaidens death

I woke up the day after his funeral feeling so upset. I sat in bed for a long time and then got up to read cards and cry a lot. I really felt the loss and was so sad that the day of honoring him and planning for him was over. I missed him so much, I just needed to be sad and feel filled with Kaiden.

After my baby died I turned a corner in my emotional journey of parenting this child. I felt some relief that the uncertainty of waiting for death was over and gratitude that my baby's quality of life was what I hoped for. my anticipatory grief served as a gradual goodbye, and with careful plans in place, I was in many ways prepared for my baby's death. I felt some regrets about certain aspects in my experience too and my grief hit hard.

it is just devastating, there are no words. some days it was almost physically painful. sadness came, for a long time. it was a deep sadness, a confused sadness, a distracted sadness. there was so much I wanted to do and just could not I had to just ride the wave.

Grieving after death

Anticipatory grieving did not erase my need to grieve after my baby died. I experienced an intense, renewed surge of grief. maybe not all right away, but as the finality of my baby's death sank in, so did the full scope of my loss. My focus shifted from looking forward to meeting and embracing my little one to looking back with intense longing.

Physical healing

After my baby died not only did I feel emotionally devastated, but I also felt physically drained. My grief caused me to feel fatigued yet still have difficulty in sleeping. My arms literally ached for my baby. In addition, I also had to recover from pregnancy and childbirth. While most of my sadness and despair attributed to my baby's death, I experienced a degree of postpartum mood swings as my hormones readjusted to pre-pregnancy levels.

I had to cope with breasts that were continuing to produce milk.

I had all the signs of recovering from pregnancy and giving birth without the reward of my baby.

I felt that I should have been able to recover quickly because there was no baby requiring around-the-clock care but adjusting to my baby's death was taxing.

My body needed extra care, as its reserves was quickly drained by grief. I deserved to take plenty of time and care to recover physically and emotionally.

It was hard for me to "take it easy", as my mam kept on reminding me to do, I had no baby to feed, or watch rest on my lap, no diapers to change. I felt as though I did not have an excuse to be tired. After all, I did not have anything to show for the very physical labor I had just gone through.

Emotional rollercoaster

After my baby died, I revisited many emotions I experienced during my pregnancy. The difference between the two was that my baby is now gone, no longer nestled in my body or arms.

Grieving is a painful but necessary process that enables you to come to terms with loss and move forward despite it.

I knew I needed to move forward and let go, but how could a mother even want to let go of their own child?, and I felt like the worst mother in the world.

I think the worst part of letting go, was letting go of all the dreams I had for Kaiden. "What would he have done if he had a full life with me?", "what would he have been like?". Those are questions that still haunt me too today. Losing my hopes and dreams for him, for us was tough.

Struggling mentally

I struggled extremely bad mentally, even months after kaidens death. I was at my lowest in life. I suffered with severe anxiety and severe panic attacks, I was diagnosed with mild depression and post-natal depression. My hair started to fall out in lumps, I was then diagnosed with alopecia areata a condition caused by trauma and stress leaving me with bald spots all over my head.

I went to counseling for a couple of weeks, but nothing could take away my pain or fill the hole that was left in my heart. It is true when

people say grief is like a rollercoaster. nothing in this world could have prepared me or anyone for that matter for what I went through at fifteen years old, an unimaginable pain.
I was all worth it for him, everything.
The first few weeks after kaidens diagnosis, never in my wildest dreams did I imagine how wonderful and rewarding this journey would be. Yes, it was painful and sorrowful, but I did not imagine the joy that was also apart of it. Kaiden has left me with so much more. I am so blessed to have lived and experienced this little life.

Pulling myself together

Three weeks after kaidens death I went back to school, I wanted to feel some sort of normality and reality. my body was there but my brain was not, I was emotionless, it was like something switched off inside of me, I end up leaving school with only one year left.

I took care of myself , I let myself grieve in my own time and a year after kaidens death I got myself my first job and I went back to school and finished my leaving cert so I could have a career in midwifery , a career in which is close to my heart and maybe one day , whilst at work , I could comfort a scared , crying mother

with empty arms just as I was and offer my knowledge to even help her in the slightest.
No one can prepare a mother for going through this, no book, or no person.
Yes, it is one hell of a journey of emotions. This sure was not the plan I had for my life, but was it worth it? absolutely !!!, do I regret it? never in a million years.
I only carried you for 33 weeks son, but I will carry you in my heart forever.

My boy, Kaiden~Rhys Paul Cooper

Printed in Great Britain
by Amazon

65610444R00137